D0127728

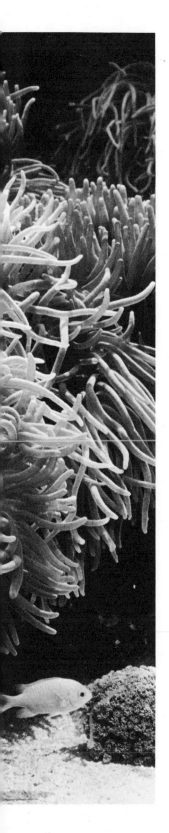

The Joy of
Snorkeling

An Illustrated Guide

AN INTERNATIONAL
OCEANOGRAPHIC
FOUNDATION
SELECTION

Steve Blount and Herb Taylor

Pisces Books
A Division of Gulf Publishing Company
Houston, Texas

The Joy of Snorkeling

Library of Congress Catalog Card Number: 83-63487

ISBN: 1-55992-000-9

Printing and binding by Toppan Printing Co. (H.K.) Ltd., Hong Kong

This book was conceived and produced by the editors of Pisces
Book Co., Inc. All the photographs in this book were taken by
the editors unless otherwise credited below. Pages 2–3, 41:
Australian Tourist Commission; p. 99: *Skin Diver* Magazine;
pp. 34–35, 40, 75 bottom left & right, 79: Fred Bavendam;
pp. 36–37: Richard Stewart; cover, pp. 39, 77, 80 bottom:
Stephen Frink; p. 78: Burton McNeely.

10   9   8   7   6   5   4   3   2

Printed in Hong Kong

Reprinted May 1989

Contents

Introduction: The Joy of Snorkeling

How can I then retrace the impression left upon me by that walk under the waters? Words are impotent to relate such wonders. . . . The light, which lit the soil thirty feet below the surface of the ocean, astonished me by its power. The solar rays shone through the watery mass easily and dissipated all color, and I clearly distinguished objects at a distance of a hundred and fifty yards. Beyond that the tints darkened into fine gradations of ultramarine, and faded into vague obscurity.

It was then ten in the morning; the rays of the sun struck the surface at rather an oblique angle, and at the touch of their light, decomposed as though through a prism, flowers, rocks, shells and polypi were shaded at the edges of the seven solar colors. It was a marvelous feast for the eyes, this complication of colored tints, a perfect kaleidoscope of green, yellow, orange, violet, indigo, and blue. . . . Various kinds of issi, clusters of pure tuft coral, prickly fungi, and anemones, formed a brilliant garden of flowers, enamelled with porphitae, decked with their collarettes of blue tentacles, sea stars studding the sandy bottom.

—Jules Verne,
Twenty Thousand Leagues Beneath the Sea

Words are indeed impotent; Frederick Dumas likened it to "the way one flies in a dream," but short of having the actual experience of diving beneath the surface of an ocean, a lake, or clear-water river, there is no way to understand the thrill of freely exploring the underwater realm.

Jules Verne had Captain Nemo and a huge machine, the *Nautilus*, as transport in his adventurous fantasy. But with only a few small aids—a face mask, swim fins, and a snorkel—you can begin snorkeling and experience this thrill for yourself.

This book will introduce you to the special techniques experienced snorkelers use to make their sport a simple, safe, enjoyable adventure. In one day

Snorkeling with friends or family enhances the joy of the sport.

you can teach yourself everything you need to know to enjoy snorkeling for a lifetime. You need buy only a quality mask, a pair of fins, and a snorkel—a kit that will take up no more room when you travel than a tennis racket and sneakers. The cost is small, and there are intriguing areas to explore anywhere there is clear water.

Unlike other outdoor recreations, snorkeling is not the sole province of the young and physically vigorous. You need not be a strong swimmer because the water will float you, and the fins will take most of the work out of moving around. Unless you have a serious heart or lung condition, you can easily become a safe, proficient snorkeler. If you need assurance, there's an easy test. Get into a bathtub filled with warm water, hold your nose tightly, and stick your head under. No panic? Fine, you'll do.

In snorkeling, you won't have to hold your nose. The mask provides a personal, portable air space in which your face, eyes, and nostrils stay dry. Through its faceplate you will see, as did Jules Verne's fictional hero, the underwater landscape clearly, sharply, and in all its subtle coloration.

Although humans have been terrestrial animals for many millions of years, we are well equipped to explore the depths. Once the initial discomfort passes, even if you've never been in the water, you'll find snorkeling natural and relaxing. Jacques Mayol, a Frenchman, has dived to more than 122 meters (400 ft.) using only basic snorkeling gear and a set of weights. You won't have to go to that extreme. One of the most proliferous reefs in the world, with six varieties of coral and thousands of tropical fish, lies at the staggering depth of half a meter.

Standing on a sandy coast, tourmaline water laps at your knees as you lower your face mask. You drop easily into the water and spread yourself out on the surface. Instantly, your weight vanishes as you glide over a shallow slope in the water, clear and slick as glycerin. The coolness envelopes you, and by its touch reveals how hot it was above. Perfectly suspended, you watch as shafts of light converge below; a brief flash reveals the star of the abyss, fire emanating from its center as from a sapphire, the color of a clear northern sky. The reflection shifts, turning about its axis with the gentle swells.

Below, the bottom is thickly cobbled. Branching staghorn coral crowns a barrow of brain coral boulders. Moving closer, the knots and knobs resolve into mini-communities: a delegation of schoolmasters confers under a purple seafan; lines of electric-blue chromis, noses pointed into a gentle current, flap like broad seagrape leaves in a calypso wind.

This is rappelling without ropes, flying without wings. You defy gravity by virtue of the similarity between the density of your body and that of the surrounding liquid. Lungs full of air, you float. Exhale and kick, and you glide from the surface toward the bottom.

Afterwards, you spread out on the beach to absorb energy from the sun, eyes closed in dreamy memory of the wonders below.

Water covers four-fifths of the globe, hiding and diffusing the details beneath. All of these waters are linked, by the rain cycle, by rivers, into one vast global ocean. The ocean is far more than a world-scale aquarium, more than a pool of dissolved minerals. The water's surface is a dividing line; below it exists a universe that has a different set of physics, a different reality from that above.

Swimming with a school of fish is an experience that is hard to match.

In a jet at cruising altitude, 10,670 meters (35,000 ft.), you are as far above the ground as a ship on the surface is from the bottom of the deepest ocean. At touchdown, 6 meters (20 ft.) above the ground, you are as close as you can get to the top of most ocean reefs without diving in. And while the broad outlines of what lies below are visible, you are still too far away to see the rainbow in a fish's eye or feel the silky texture of a turtle's back. You can't explore a forest from the air; you have to get down among the trees. You can't know the ocean by sailing on its surface; you must dive in.

Snorkeling is a simple set of skills, a unique mode of transport in a world every bit as different from your front yard as the asteroid belt between Mars and Jupiter. The water atmosphere is different: 800 times denser than air, it reduces your perceived weight to one-seventh Earth-normal or less. Water is the only place this side of the ionosphere where true weightlessness can be achieved. For this reason, astronauts train under water.

The inhabitants are different: animals that look like rocks, plants that look like animals—a petting zoo of protein so complex that, even as geneticists create new forms of life in the laboratory, marine scientists can only guess which kingdoms some aquatic creatures belong to.

The topography is different, encompassing every known terrestrial form from sand flats to cliffs to impossibly tall mountains, to some, like the Mariannas Trench, 11 km (7 mi.) deep, that are unknown above water. If you're looking for pleasurable and exotic adventure, look here. Mount Everest would fit wholly within the Trench, and its peak, covered by a mile of seawater, would be obscured.

Beyond seeing and discovering, there is another dimension to snorkeling—that of sensation. Humans and other mammals have a genetically determined response to the increased pressure our bodies

Once you experience the underwater world, you will want to share it with others. Underwater photography is one of the best ways of communicating your experiences to others.

experience under water. Called the mammalian diving reflex, it triggers extraordinary physical changes that make snorkeling easier and more enjoyable. As pressure increases, the reflex reroutes much of the blood, and the oxygen it carries, from the extremities to the torso and especially to the brain. The extra oxygen, combined with the snorkeler's deep, repetitious breathing and the sensation of weightlessness, produce an almost trancelike calm.

Most snorkelers are convinced they've found their magic kingdom; it's just seaward of the next reef, waiting for their next dive. The ocean is their wilderness, big enough to swallow their fantasies whole.

Snorkeling is an ideal activity for one, two, or an entire family. Water greatly reduces the differences size can play in physical ability. Women, who have a greater percentage of body fat and more strongly developed legs, excel at snorkeling, often outperforming men of similar size and weight. Children gain confidence quickly as the mask eliminates the problem of getting water in the nose, and become better, safer swimmers after learning to snorkel. For even the youngest, quality gear is available in very small sizes.

Especially in tropical ocean areas, entire vacations can be organized around snorkeling. It provides excitement, a chance to learn more about the foreign place that you are visiting, plenty of sun, and an absorbing, relaxing activity. Pleasantly invigorating, snorkeling won't tire you out and you'll be eager to pursue other activities on land.

At most resort locations around the world, there are guides who can tell you where to find the best spots for snorkeling. Or, you may be able to arrange a guided tour from a snorkeling boat, taking in the shallow areas surrounding offshore islands or shallow patch reefs in the open ocean. In many places, including the Grenadine Islands in the Caribbean, California's Channel Islands, Australia's Great Barrier Reef, and the Greek islands you can arrange single- or multi-day sailing trips that will include stops at choice snorkeling locations. Ask a travel agent or national and tourism offices for complete information. If you'd rather go it alone, Chapter 3 will show you how to use a map and a navigational chart to find good snorkeling areas.

Once you've learned the basics, you'll want to expand your activities to free-diving (diving beneath the surface without scuba gear), hand-feeding fish, photography, shell-collecting, or even scuba diving.

If you're ready, the fun begins on the next page.

Identifying fish, corals, and crawling creatures can become a totally consuming pastime.

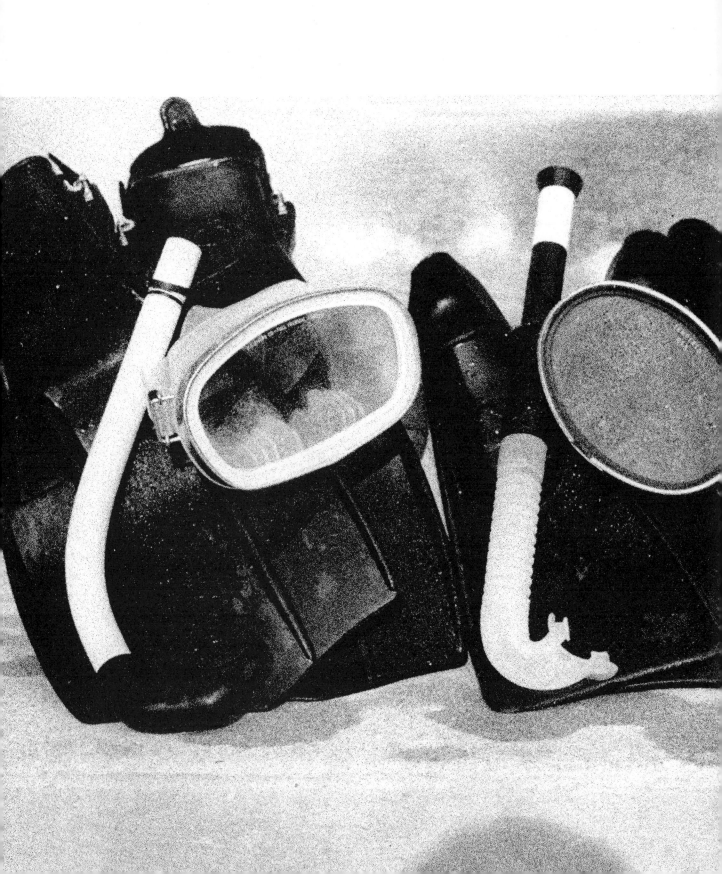

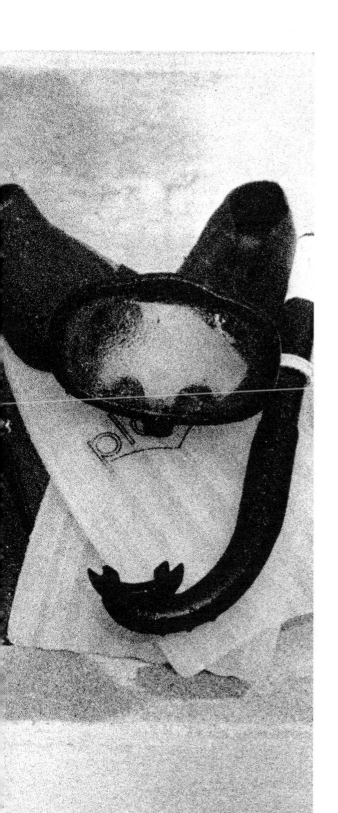

Getting The Right Stuff

MASKS

To snorkel comfortably, you must be able to see, to breathe, and to move about freely. The mask, fins, and snorkel are your passport into the fantastic world beneath the surface. The mask keeps water away from your eyes, enabling you to see clearly. The fins help you move almost effortlessly through the water. The snorkel lets you breathe without lifting your head above the surface.

To get the most pleasure from snorkeling, it is important that these three items be of the best quality. This will make them a bit more expensive, but averaged out over the years of pleasure they will bring, the cost is small.

Water is more dense than air. That is, given equal volumes of air and water, the water weighs much more. When light waves move through a material of one density into a material of a different density, the waves are bent radically at the place where the tow materials meet; this is called refraction. The lenses of our eyes were designed to focus light moving from air into the tissues of the eye. Light moving from *water* into the eyes is bent more severely, and this is why you can't see clearly when you open your eyes under water. The mask traps air between your eyes and the water, allowing you to see clearly through the glass faceplate. The mask also provides comfort

A well-made mask will incorporate all the features identified and be made of rubber soft enough to conform to your facial features.

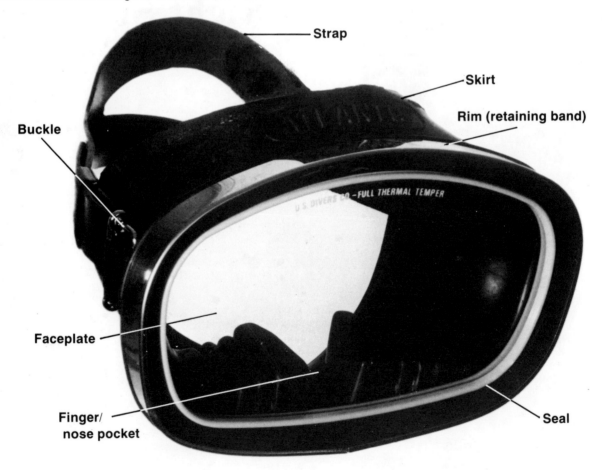

Strap

Skirt

Rim (retaining band)

Buckle

U.S. DIVERS CO - FULL THERMAL TEMPER

Faceplate

Finger/
nose pocket

Seal

by keeping water away from your eyes and out of your nose.

As you submerge, the water will press against the mask. The farther down you go, the harder the water will press. Because the mask covers your nose as well as your eyes, you will be able to breathe a little air into the mask through your nose to keep the mask from cutting into your face. This is called *equalizing pressure* in the mask (for a full explanation of pressure and equalization see pages 50–51).

While swimming goggles also allow you to see under water they do not keep your nose dry and *must not* be used for snorkeling if you intend to dive below the surface. Goggles cannot be equalized, and if you dive below the surface, they will cut into the sensitive skin on your face, perhaps even rupturing blood vessels around your eyes. Buy a mask.

Parts of the mask

The typical mask (see photo) has a glass faceplate and a frame to hold the glass in place. The frame may be made of rubber, plastic, metal, or a combination of these. The skirt extends back from the frame and seals against the face, holding the faceplate away from the face and keeping water out of the resulting air space. The nose pocket (or finger pockets if indented into the skirt) must be of a size and shape that will allow you to pinch your nostrils closed while underwater. The strap attaches to buckles on both sides. Inside, a feather-edge seal helps keep out water.

Types of masks

Masks come in various shapes, each with its own advantages. Broadly speaking, masks can be categorized as oval, wrap-around, frog-eye, or low-volume. Manufacturers have many names for their masks—prismatic, tri-window, and so on—but all will fit generally into these categories. Faces come in all sizes and shapes; try many masks on until you find the type that feels most comfortable.

(Top to bottom) Oval mask; wrap-around mask; frog-eye mask; child's mask.

To find out if a mask fits you properly, press it against your face without placing the strap behind your head, then inhale. If the mask has formed an airtight seal, the suction will keep it in place without your having to hold it up. If it falls away quickly, it is too small or the wrong shape for your face and will leak water while you are snorkeling.

Oval. The oval was the first type of mask. As its name suggests, it is oval in shape often with low internal volume (small air space inside the mask). The lower its volume, the easier a mask is to equalize while diving below the surface. If you have a broad face, some oval sizes may fit you well.

Wrap-around. The wrap-around mask has a faceplate that extends back toward the ears, to allow the wearer some peripheral vision. The faceplate may be a single, curved piece. It may consist of a flat front window and two smaller windows let into the skirt of the mask. The wrap-around is popular with scuba divers, but because it generally has a large air space inside, more air is required to equalize it as you descend.

Frog-eye. The frog-eye mask is shaped much like a set of goggles, but with a pocket which drops down to enclose the nose. The faceplate is divided into two teardrop-shaped lenses which may or may not be connected across the bridge of the nose. Frog-eye masks generally have a low internal volume, and the glass fits close to the eyes, which allows greater peripheral vision.

Low Volume. Low volume masks require very little air to equalize their pressure. This makes them ideal for snorkelers who make deep dives from the surface. Low volume masks come in various shapes, but most are oval or frog-eye. Extremely low volume masks are, in some ways, less comfortable than slightly larger masks of similar design.

Materials

The most comfortable masks are made of soft, natural rubber. However, sunlight and skin oils cause pure rubber to deteriorate quickly. Synthetic rubber is long-lasting, but it's stiff and uncomfortable to wear. The best mask is a compromise. Comfort is paramount; a stiff mask held against your face by an oversized rubber band can drive you out of the water quickly. Unless the mask is pure gum rubber, you can bet it has some synthetic rubber in it. Get a mask that is soft and pliable, but which has some synthetics to prolong its life. If you can't bend the skirt double by pinching it between your thumb and forefinger, it's probably too stiff to wear for an hour at a time.

Some manufacturers are making masks out of silicone, a soft synthetic compound which seems to be very comfortable. The skirt of a silicone mask is generally clear or translucent, which also admits more light inside the mask. In addition, the silicone masks are hypo-allergenic, a must if you have sensitive skin.

The faceplate of your mask must be made of tempered glass, and the word "tempered" will be marked on the plate if it is.

Construction

A good mask will have a well-crafted look. The seams of the rubber will be smooth. The parts will fit together without gaps. The feather-edge seal will stand at least 0.6 cm (¼ in.) away from the inside of the skirt, and you should be able to see a slight rippling or feathering along its forward edge. If a mask does not have this seal, it is inferior and water will leak in continuously.

The buckles may be made of plastic or metal. The metal buckles tend to rust after use, but this doesn't affect their performance. Check to see that you can tighten or loosen the strap easily. The strap also should have ribs on the underside at the ends where it goes through the buckles to keep it from slipping.

A good fit

The right mask is the one that fits your face comfortably and keeps water out. If not properly fitted, even a quality mask will leak. Try different styles of masks, pressing them against your face without the strap in place until you find one that is the right size, feels comfortable, and looks good to you.

Feel around the edges of the mask while it is against your face. Make sure the skirt touches your skin all the way around, especially at the temples. A mask that is too large will extend beyond the temples, while one that is too small will not extend above the gap at the bridge of the nose or beyond the outer corners of the eyes. Push the mask firmly against your face, inhale through your nose, and let go of the mask. If the mask is sealing properly, the slight vacuum inside will hold it firmly against your face for at least ten seconds. If the mask does not seal, you will feel air leaking back in and the mask will quickly drop from your face.

The lock feature on this mask is very effective because of the tension created by the rubber projection on the mask and the ridges on the strap.

This mask incorporates a number of important features. When selecting a mask, look for a double skirt for good sealing, an equalizing device, a split headstrap, and a positive lock to secure the strap in position.

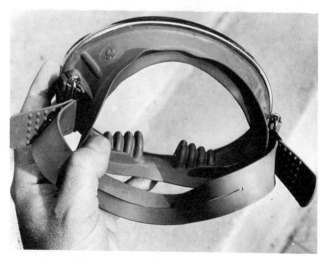

VISION

Everything you see under water through the mask will be magnified and will appear about 25 percent closer. If you have slight vision problems, this may be all the help you'll need. If you have more severe problems, there are a number of solutions.

One inexpensive solution is to purchase a set of plastic frames designed to hold a pair of conventional glass lenses inside the mask. This may be the best solution for extreme nearsightedness or astigmatism.

It is also possible to have an optician make lenses to your own prescription and bond them to your faceplate. A store that sells scuba diving equipment will probably know of a local optician who is equipped to handle this.

If you wear contact lenses, you should be able to wear them while snorkeling with no difficulty. It is possible, though, to lose them if they wash out before you put on your mask, or if your mask accidentally fills with water. Be sure you have an extra pair. Generally, soft lenses are more comfortable than hard lenses as they conform easily to the slight changes that occur in the shape of the eyes when they are subjected to pressures while diving.

One easy fix for poor vision is to buy a mask with an optically correct faceplate. Several manufacturers offer masks with faceplates that correct vision in various strengths, in both plus and minus diopters. Ask your optometrist or optician what your prescription is in diopters, then select a mask with the proper strength faceplate. If your vision in one eye differs markedly from that in the other eye, a correctable frog-eye mask will let you mix and match lens strengths.

If you intend to buy an optically correctable mask, you will find a larger selection at stores that specialize in scuba diving equipment.

Masks made of silicone are hypo-allergenic. If your skin is very sensitive, try one of this type.

Diopter masks have specially ground eyepieces which will correct nearsightedness or farsightedness.

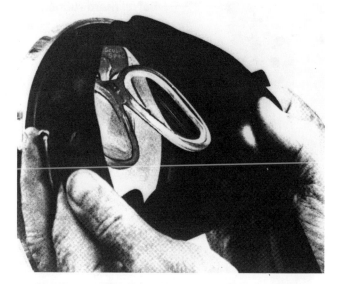

Using an insert with corrected lenses is an inexpensive solution to seeing clearly under water.

Corrective lenses can be bonded with an optical glue to the inside of almost any mask.

SNORKELS

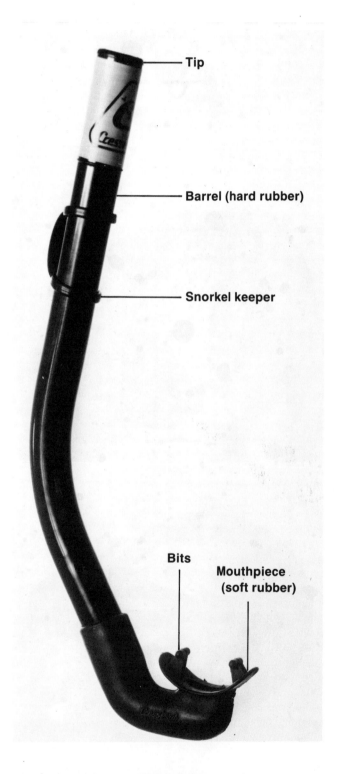

Tip

Barrel (hard rubber)

Snorkel keeper

Bits

Mouthpiece (soft rubber)

The snorkel is simply a tube through which you can draw air while under water, but it deserves no less attention than the mask. Water is more dense than air, and it exerts much greater pressure on the body. Even at a depth of just 30 cm (12 in.), there are 200 pounds of pressure on a diver's chest, making it nearly impossible to draw air through a tube using only lung power. The ideal snorkel is relatively short, 23–35 cm (9–14 in.) above the mouthpiece. Since you breathe only at the surface, the snorkel need only be long enough to extend a few inches above water when you are floating face down.

Choose a snorkel as carefully as you would a mask. Comfort is the key element.

Types of snorkels

J-Tube. Snorkels are differentiated by their shape. The simplest is the J-tube, but this is not highly recommended for serious snorkelers. The rigid J shape requires a longer barrel to lift the open tip as far above the water as a shorter flex or wrap-around snorkel. The shorter the tube, the easier it is to breathe through.

Flex. The flex snorkel has a straight upper tube with a rubber accordion-pleat section connecting the barrel to the mouthpiece. The flex is very comfortable for some people as the mouthpiece hangs straight down, away from the face, when not in use. Flex snorkels are slightly harder to clear (see pages 48–49) than J or wrap-around snorkels because small drops of water may collect in the accordion pleats. These pleats also tend to wear out over time and develop small holes that let water in.

Wrap-around. The wrap-around is the choice of most serious snorkelers. Its curves hug the face and head, so it needs only a short tube to keep the tip above the water. Wrap-around snorkels are available with advanced features such as a rotating mouthpiece for comfortable positioning, and a moldable mouthpiece bit (see below). The cost of a superior wrap-around is only a little more than a cheap, plastic J-tube. It is your lifeline to the surface; buy a good one.

Simple J-tube snorkel with full-bite mouthpiece.

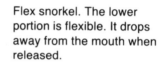
Flex snorkel. The lower portion is flexible. It drops away from the mouth when released.

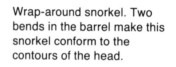
Wrap-around snorkel. Two bends in the barrel make this snorkel conform to the contours of the head.

Fit

Remember, you'll be face down when using your snorkel, so when trying a snorkel for size and fit, the tip does not go above your head but *behind* it, almost directly behind your mouth.

The barrel should curve out from the mouthpiece, cross parallel with the cheek bone, cross the ear at a 90-degree angle, then go straight back or curve slightly in toward the center of the head.

It is easiest to get a good fit in a flex because the accordion pleats twist with little effort. If you choose a J or wrap-around, hold the barrel against your head and check that the mouthpiece falls directly in front of your mouth. If you have to stretch to get the bit in your mouth, your jaw muscles are going to tire quickly in the water.

Materials

The best snorkels are made of rubber/synthetic rubber compounds. Plastic is not a good material for snorkels as it tends to crack after exposure to sun. Squeeze the barrel; it should flex easily as you squeeze. Some very good snorkels are made of silicone, the clear or translucent synthetic compound.

Parts of the snorkel

The snorkel (see photo) is comprised of the tip, or opening, where the air enters; the barrel, or tube, which carries air down; and the mouthpiece, which has bits you hold in your teeth and a seal that fits between your teeth and lips to keep water out.

When trying snorkels, remember that the mouthpiece must fit comfortably in your mouth when the tip of the snorkel is almost directly behind your mouth—not above your head.

Big bore or small bore?

In addition to the length, the diameter (or bore) of the snorkel barrel affects how easy it is to breathe through. It is easiest to breathe through a short, large bore snorkel than through one with a long, large bore, a short, small bore, or a long, small bore. A larger bore requires a little more effort to clear, but by keeping to a short barrel, this disadvantage can be reduced. Generally, an average-sized adult will breathe best with a snorkel about 2.5 cm (1 in.) in diameter. Small children will be more comfortable clearing a snorkel 2.0 cm (¾ in.) in diameter or even smaller. A very large man with strong lungs may need a bore up to 1.27 cm (½ in.).

The size, shape, and material of the mouthpiece are critical to your comfort. First, check to make sure the mouthpiece is soft and pliable, and that there are no rough edges. Do not buy a snorkel with a plastic mouthpiece. Plastic tastes bad and is very uncomfortable. The seal should fit comfortably in your lips without rubbing the crease where lips and gums join. Ideally, the seal should cover at least half the length of your front teeth, top and bottom.

A mouthpiece that's too big or too small, or hard to hold, is going to tire your jaws long before the rest of you is ready to leave the water. Use of a moldable bit is strongly recommended. Moldable bits are soft plastic pieces that fit over the regular rubber bits. Before using a moldable bit, soften it in boiling water. Then remove it, slip it onto the snorkel mouthpiece, put it in your mouth, and bite down. The moldable bit will conform to the shape of your teeth, and this helps you keep a better grip on the snorkel without straining your jaws.

Snorkel keeper

You may want to simply slip the barrel of the snorkel under your mask strap while snorkeling, but a number of small devices are available to attach the snorkel to the strap. If you tuck the barrel under the strap, it may rub against your face or slip out and get lost. A snorkel keeper is recommended, the simpler the device, the better.

These snorkel-keepers are typical, simple designs. More complicated keepers do not work any better and may get tangled in your hair while you are snorkeling.

This snorkel has moldable bits on the mouthpiece. When boiled, the bits soften. Biting down on the soft bits gives them the imprint of your teeth, making it easier and more comfortable to grip the mouthpiece in your teeth.

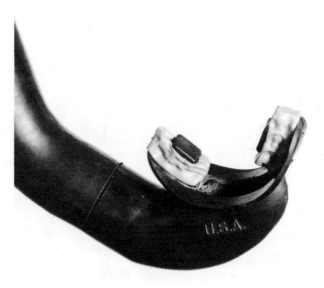

FINS

Ideally, your fins will do much of the work of moving you through the water. There are two basic types of fins: open-heel and full-foot. Open-heel fins have adjustable straps that go behind the heel to hold the fin on. Full-foot fins have fully enclosed pockets like a regular shoe. At one time, full-foot fins were for swimming only, and open-heel fins were only for scuba diving, but new models have made this distinction obsolete.

Open-heel fins

Open-heel fins generally can withstand the stress of a more rigid blade, and they give a great deal of forward thrust when you push them very hard. This advantage is offset by the fact that when they are pushed through the water, open-heel fins place a considerable amount or stress across the arch and instep of the foot. This stress can cause cramps in the arch of the foot, and the stiff blade can bring on muscle fatigue quickly. The adjustable heel strap will allow you to wear neoprene boots to help keep your feet warm in cold water; in fact, you may need to wear boots to keep the strap from chafing your heel—even thick socks are not enough to protect uncalloused heels from fin straps. Unless you have very strong legs or are accustomed to open-heel fins, you'll be better off with full-foot fins.

Open-heel fins are very popular, but it is a good idea to use them in conjunction with a pair of hard-soled neoprene booties. The booties will protect the heel of your foot should it be necessary to stand on coral or a rocky bottom.

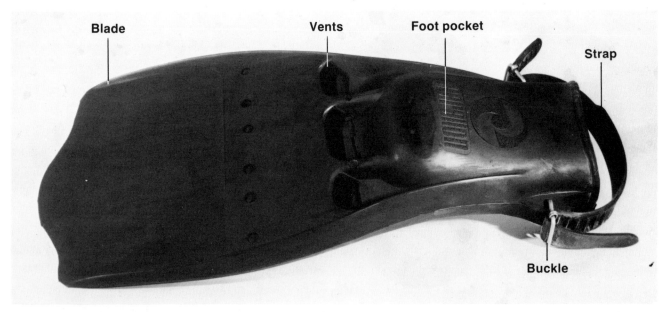

Blade   Vents   Foot pocket   Strap   Buckle

Full-foot fins

Full-foot fins distribute the stress of propulsion evenly over the entire foot, and with a large blade, can provide nearly as much thrust as a stiff, open-heel fin. If you plan to wear neoprene boots, buy full-foot fins several sizes larger than your normal shoe size. How much larger depends upon the thickness of the neoprene. A fin two or three sizes larger than your shoe size will accommodate a boot made from 4.5 mm (³⁄₁₆ in.) neoprene; a boot of 6 mm (¼ in.) neoprene will require three or four extra sizes.

What size blade?

In a full-foot fin, the larger the blade, the faster you'll go. A long, *flexible* blade will give optimum efficiency; it will give you enough power for any situation without causing much fatigue. In an open-heel fin, a great deal of thrust can be developed by a small, stiff blade. The many open-heel fins with flow-through vents are very satisfactory.

Materials

A blend of several rubber/synthetic compounds is necessary to make a quality fin. Plastic compounds are not good for fins; no quality fins are all plastic.

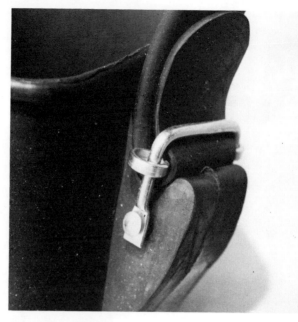

A positive locking device is an important feature for fins with adjustable straps. Once straps are properly adjusted, there should be no need to readjust them because of slipping.

Full-pocket fins are very comfortable when they fit properly. Improper fit can lead to chafing and blisters, so check carefully for correct fit.

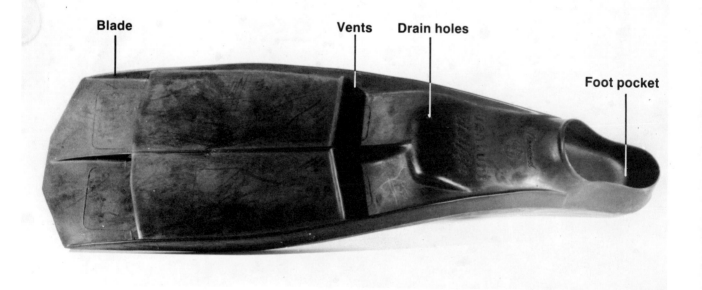

Blade   **Vents**   **Drain holes**   **Foot pocket**

Getting Started

GEAR UP

Having carefully selected a set of comfortable gear, you should try everything on at home, clean the mask, and adjust the various straps. Wash the faceplate of the mask thoroughly with warm water and liquid dishwashing soap and dry it. To put on the mask hold it in one hand, grasping the sides with your thumb and another finger so your hand spans the front of the faceplate. From the front of the mask, slip the other hand under the strap so that the strap rests across the back of the hand, palm toward your face. Raise the mask and position it on your face; then stretch the strap up and back, passing the palm of your hand over the top of your head. (By placing your hand between your head and the strap, you prevent the rubber strap from catching and pulling your hair.) Hold the strap in place with the hand that first held the mask and release the other hand.

The mask should be snug, but not so tight that it causes deep creases in the face, or pain. If the straps are too loose or too tight, remove the mask and adjust the straps, making certain you adjust each side equally, so the wide part of the strap remains centered behind your head. Further adjustment may be necessary once you get in the water.

Snorkel

Take the mask off and attach the snorkel holder and snorkel to the strap just where it crosses your temple. The snorkel can be worn on either side, whichever feels most comfortable to you. Once it's attached, put the mask back on and check that the mouthpiece reaches your mouth easily, adjusting the snorkel up or down in the holder to suit.

Fins

Both full-foot and open-heel fins go on the same way. If you'll be wearing neoprene boots, put those on first. While seated, slip your feet as far as possible into the pocket of the fin. With full-foot fins, slide two fingers under your heel and stretch the rubber

When putting on the mask, use the back of your hand to stretch the strap up and slide it over your head. This will keep the rubber strap from pulling your hair as you slip it on.

pocket until your heel slips down into it. With open-heel fins, pull the strap back and slide it up over the back of your heel.

Fins always go on easier when they are wet. If you are just trying them on, walking is difficult, particularly in the water. The proper way to walk with fins on is to walk backwards. Looking over one shoulder, slowly shuffle backwards. Don't try to lift your feet off the floor as this will unbalance you. Walking with fins is easier if you do it with a buddy. Link arms, and using each other to balance, shuffle backwards together.

The first few times

Especially until you become experienced, the most pleasurable places to snorkel will have clear, calm water, little or no current, and something to see under water. If you feel particularly clumsy with the mask, fins, and snorkel, you may want to try your first lessons in a swimming pool. The controlled environment may provide extra confidence. Otherwise, a clear lake or pond, or a tranquil stretch of ocean in a protected bay will make an exciting place to start.

Choosing a site

The most important considerations when you choose a place to snorkel are the water conditions that prevail at the site: temperature, visibility, depth, currents, boat traffic, and wave action.

You'll also need to consider shore conditions: an entry and exit point, structures such as piers or jetties, rocks or other obstructions, and the presence of fishermen.

Obviously, you'll need a clear entry point. This should be a sandy stretch where the shallow water is relatively clear of rocks or coral. If there are currents that will pull you away from the entry point, or if you don't want to swim in a large circle, also choose and check out a clear exit before getting in. If possible, survey the snorkel site from above—a bluff, the top of an auto, or the roof of a building. You'll be able to observe entry and exit and water conditions much better from a high spot.

If there are a number of fishermen in the area, find another spot. Aside from the possibility of getting hooked, you could become entangled in the long, transparent fishing lines. Although a great

variety of marine life can be found under or attached to piers, trash such as tires, broken bottles, wire, old fishing line, nets, and cans is usually abundant too. In tropical areas, pilings and cross-members under a pier may be covered with sharp barnacle shells or stinging fire coral (see pages 66–69).

Jetties—structures that project into the water to shield an area from waves—are usually made of piles of large rocks. Waves on the outside of a jetty can throw you against those rocks. Also, be aware that wherever any structure interrupts the flow of water, a current or other strong movement of water is likely.

The first time you snorkel, you will probably have to stop and adjust your mask strap and the position of your snorkel a couple of times until you are comfortable.

WATER CONDITIONS

Temperature and visibility

Water chills the body much faster than air. Even water as warm as 29C (85°F) may feel cool after a short time. Individual tolerance to cold varies tremendously, but generally, you'll be uncomfortable in water much below 21°C (70°F). (See pages 100–101 for information on protection from cold.) Ocean temperatures can generally be obtained from a local newspaper's meteorological guide, which may also provide information on tides and approaching weather. In most bodies of water, you can distinguish different layers of water temperature. The colder water, which is denser, sinks. So even if the surface feels tepid or warm, expect the temperature 3-6 meters (10-20 ft.) below the surface to be as much as 8C (15°F) cooler.

One purpose of the mask is to allow you to see. Snorkeling in low-visibility water is neither fun nor safe. Find a clear body of water with 3 meters (10 ft.) or more of visibility. Stay away from harbors, muddy rivers, run-off areas, and the like.

Waves

Waves are nearly always present in oceans or large lakes. With your snorkel, you'll be able to swim safely in moderate waves, 0.5–1.0 meters (2-3 ft.) high. Avoid higher waves, unless you'll simply be snorkeling through them to get to an area of calmer water.

The water in a wave does not travel forward. Actually, the wave travels through the water, causing the water particles to move up and down as it passes. The shape and movement of waves can tell you a lot about the bottom shape, and about which directions currents or rips may be moving (see illustration).

Using currents

Incoming tides and wave action move water toward the shore. The water must then somehow return to the sea. When the return flow is along the bottom, under the waves, it is called *undertow*. Undertow sucks surface water—and floating objects such as snorkelers—toward the bottom and out to sea. A beach with a bottom that slopes evenly away from shore is likely to have a strong undertow at times of maximum tidal flow in or out, or when breakers are especially large. This type of beach can be recognized by a consistent wave pattern with only one line of breaking waves. Unless you're a strong swimmer and know how to handle an undertow without panicking, avoid this type of situation.

A beach with two lines of breakers, one far out, one close in, indicates a bar or reef offshore at the farthest line of breakers. Between the two breakers is a trough. The water in the trough will be moving toward a place where it can exit through a break in the bar. A rapid current toward and through a break in a bar is called a *rip*. A rip area can sometimes be seen as a flatter area in a line of breakers moving over an offshore bar. Experienced snorkelers sometimes use rips as a way to get out beyond the breakers quickly. Once through the bar, the rip generally slows down and dissipates quickly. However, unless you know exactly what you're doing, avoid rips, as they will carry you out to sea.

A particularly vicious type of rip occurs at the narrow mouths of circular bays or tropical lagoons. When the tide runs in or out, the current in the narrow channel can be several knots. Even with fins, you will not be able to swim faster than one knot, and a fast current will surely take you where it's going.

At a beach where waves strike the shore at an angle, there may be an along shore-current where the water moves parallel to the beach. Use this type of current to travel down the beach in the direction of the water flow. Walk up the beach a distance against the current; then enter and let the current carry you to the spot where you want to exit.

Swim across current

Beach formations and various obstructions in the water will cause currents (see illustration). Keep these in mind and use the movement of the water to make your snorkeling easier and safer. Do not fight currents. Struggling against even a mild current will tire you unnecessarily. If caught in an undesirable current, *swim at an angle across the current* aiming for a point or toward a projection in the shoreline.

The diagrams shown here (from the NOAA Diving Manual) illustrate a variety of shore types and currents. The "E's" indicate entry points and the "X's" are points for exits.

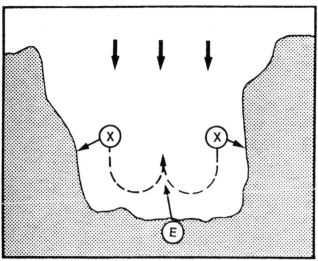

Small Deep Coves

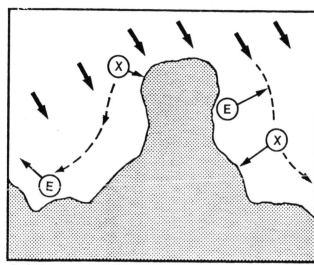

Points

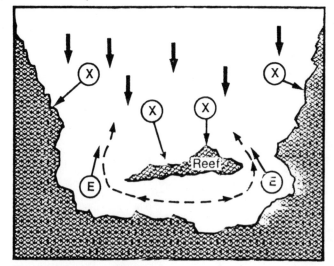

Rocky Cove – Reefs

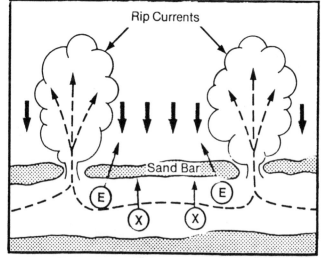

Sand Bar – Sandy Beach – Rip Current

USING A MAP AND MARINE CHART

If you are traveling, the best way to find good snorkeling spots is by talking to local divers or fishermen, asking the location of shallow reefs or clear water areas. Failing that, a map and nautical chart can be used. The charts won't tell you about current or visibility, but otherwise are good indicators.

You'll need a topographic map, a marine chart, tide charts, and some information about the prevailing winds (direction the wind ordinarily blows from, and how hard). The charts and map can usually be bought at marinas or at the harbor master's office in a port.

Use the topographic map to check the beach elevation. Is the area bounded by sheer cliffs, sloping hills, or flat beaches? You'll need some beach area to enter and exit. Also, stay away from the mouths of streams or rivers that flow into the ocean as these carry silt which clouds the water.

An ideal snorkeling area would be a cove or bay that has a sharp cusp sheltering the water from the prevailing winds. The wind, and the waves it generates, will break against this cusp, leaving the bay waters calm. An area in the lee (or downside) of an arm of land that projects into the ocean is good also.

The marine chart will show you where coral or rock reefs are. It will also give depths in fathoms or meters. (One fathom equals 1.85 meters or 6 ft.)

By reading depth indications on the marine chart, you will see whether the ocean bottom is even or uneven, how far out the reefs are and how deep they are. Study the chart, looking for paths water will take through the area, up to the beach, away from or around obstructions. If there are any shipwrecks in the area, they will be marked.

Studying a few marine charts, especially from tropical areas, will show you how reefs grow. Coral

A marine chart yields valuable information to the snorkeler as well as the boater. This section of Nautical Chart 11451 issued by the National Oceanic and Atmospheric Administration covers part of the Florida Keys. The small numbers scattered all over the chart are the depths in feet at low tide. There are many symbols, each with a distinct meaning on this section of chart, but briefly, crosses or asterisks surrounded by dots are rocks, while elongated ovals with large crosses inside are shipwrecks. Note that on the south side of Plantation Key, the area labeled The Rocks is a promising snorkel area. Although it is about 1,000 yards offshore, it is very shallow and has an old shipwreck and an abundance of coral, as indicated by the notations for the rocks and the legend "co," which stands for coral.

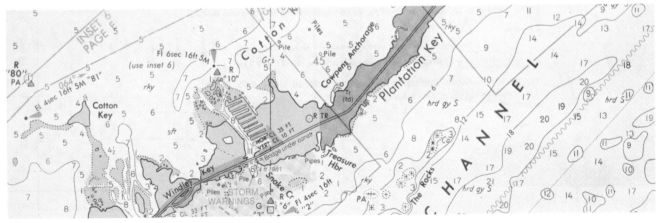

type, wave action, bottom contour, and current all play a part in forming a reef. Where the chart indicates small, separated clumps of coral scattered about with no pattern, you are likely to find still water and flat, shallow sand bottom. You may see two rows of coral running parallel to shore, one in shallow water, one deeper. Here you may find a beach with two sets of breakers and a rip current. If the outermost reef is a good distance from the inner one with a wide, shallow plain between, this will provide a very calm, lagoon-like setting. Where a wide, shallow shelf drops suddenly to 18 or 21 meters (60 to 70 ft.), then rapidly again to 45 meters (150 ft.), you'll find what divers call a "wall," or undersea cliff. Inshore of that cliff the water will usually be very clear, as it is continually replenished by clear water from the deeps. Large fish and vigorous coral growth normally occur near these walls. The inshore reefs often run perpendicular to shore, directly out to the wall in long, finger-like barrows.

A word of caution about charts and maps—particularly of areas outside the industrialized nations—is that they are not always accurate when they are made, and conditions in water areas can change quickly. Although we've come a long way since the days when mariner's maps were marked with the legend "here be monsters" just west of the Straits of Gibraltar, relying on everything to be just as it's pictured on a map is asking the impossible. In areas subject to wave action (including large lakes and rivers), sandbars and shoals move constantly. Check every important feature in your snorkel area visually before going in. Don't assume that because the map shows a bar or shoal in a certain position, that it will affect area currents according to the textbook theory of water movement.

Ask local marine or wildlife officers about your tentative snorkel area, and inquire about alternatives. Their knowledge of an area and its possibilities is often far greater than what you can extract from a map or guidebook.

A topographic map can also be of use to a snorkeler. It can give you a clear idea of how to approach a particular area and also of what to expect in the water. Topographic maps of the United States are issued by the Department of Interior Geological Survey. This map (Bayville Quadrangle) shows a portion of the North Shore of Long Island in New York State. The dots and asterisks near Oak Neck Beach indicate a rocky area in shallow water—an interesting area for snorkeling.

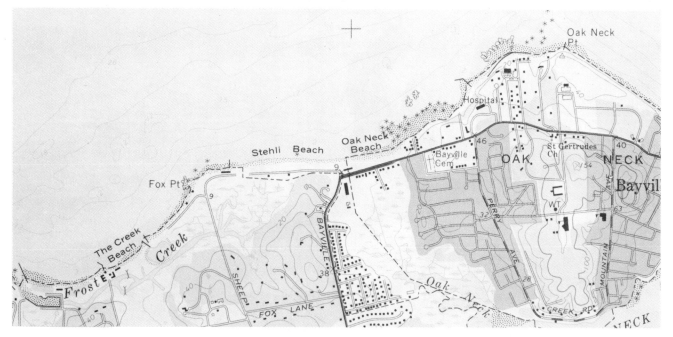

SNORKELING FROM SHORE VS. SNORKELING FROM A BOAT

Until you feel competent as a snorkeler and confident in the water, you will be safest snorkeling in areas that can be reached by swimming out from shore, rather than snorkeling from a boat. Unless you are with a professional operator of diving and snorkeling tours, the operation of a boat brings additional responsibilities which complicate your outing. For example, a boat should never be left anchored and unattended. Even well-anchored craft have been known to wander away on their own when no one is in them. At least two people will have to stay in the boat at all times: one capable of operating the boat and one capable of saving any snorkeler in the party who gets into trouble. And in case someone does get into trouble, a stretch of beach is a lot bigger target to get to than a boat, which may not even be visible to a panicky swimmer at water level in moderate swells. Properly equipping

a boat for safe snorkeling or diving is beyond the scope of this book, but few private boat owners go to the trouble to have the necessary gear—a long trail line with buoy that can be let out of the stern to float downcurrent, a swimstep or ladder, a powerful VHF marine radio, and oxygen and other medical supplies, just to name a few.

Psychologically, it is comforting to most people to have dry land close at hand and a shallow bottom under their feet while learning anything new in the water.

Once you master the sport of snorkeling, you may want to explore offshore sites. A small inflatable dinghy, such as this one from Avon, can make getting to an offshore snorkeling area easy.

When possible, view snorkeling areas from a cliff, hill or other high place before going in and note evidence of currents, landmarks, entrance and possible exit points. (Right) A view of this site from a rock ledge reveals a wide, shallow bay. The dark brown spots, as at the bottom of the photo, are large stands of elkhorn coral. The light green areas indicate white sand bottom. (Below) The view from a hill shows this site to be ideal. The white strip just behind the two snorkelers in the water indicates a clean, sandy bottom free of rocks, coral or sea urchins. The large, dark patch in the immediate foreground and the oval patch in the center of the photo is seaweed, not coral. The brown patch that begins at the left center of the photo is coral, however. The wave breaking on top of that patch indicates something hard — coral — close to the surface. With practice you'll learn to make the distinctions. The solid line of breakers in the background indicates a coral reef running more or less parallel with the beach. Note that the water inshore of the reef is light green, while that to seaward is dark blue. This indicates a shallow, sandy shelf running out to the reef with a fairly sharp dropoff on the other side. (Overleaf) An elevated view shows The Baths, a site on Virgin Gorda in the British Virgin Islands, to be protected, calm and shallow. Note how the texture of the rocks beneath the water differs from that of the submerged coral seen in the photo on this page, below. The gradual darkening of the water from green in the foreground to dark blue out where the boats are anchored shows the bottom has a gradual slope, as opposed to the sharp dropoff seen at a reef line.

(Preceding pages) Large rounded brain coral boulders and jagged fronds of elkhorn coral entrance visitors to Buck Island Reef National Monument on St. Croix, U.S. Virgin Islands. (Below) Temperate waters also offer exciting opportunities to observe underwater life and activity if you look closely. Because these waters are not as clear as in the tropics, stay in shallow areas for best visibility. You might want to wear a wetsuit jacket, or even a full suit, to keep warm. (Facing page) Wearing gloves is a sensible precaution against common marine hazards like sharp coral. The large encrusted objects in this photo are an anchor (foreground) and cannon (background) salvaged from a Spanish treasure fleet that sank off the east coast of Florida in 1715. Removed from wreck sites off Fort Pierce, Florida, these artifacts can be seen by snorkelers visiting John Pennekamp Coral Reef State Park in Key Largo, Florida.

Australia's Barrier Reef is dotted with hundreds of tiny pools and pockets that are ideal sites for snorkeling. Of course, you don't have to go that far to find small tidal pools that are filled with fascinating marine creatures.

(Facing page) When the right site is chosen, snorkeling can be an ideal family activity. Remember that the difficulty of swimming to the site and the difficulty of the excursion itself must be well within the physical abilities of the smallest, youngest, or weakest member of the group. Shallow, inshore sites, such as this one at Buck Island, St. Croix, in the American Virgin Islands, are ideal. An underwater nature trail, complete with markers describing the surroundings, is maintained here by the National Park Service.

Snorkel Swimming

FLOATING AND BREATHING

Once you have a calm site to practice in, it's time to get in the water. With your mask, fins, and snorkel in place, walk backward out into shallow water. Kneel in the water and make sure your mask is secure. Take the snorkel in your mouth and check that the barrel and tip are in the right position. Now, lean forward, plug the mouthpiece of the snorkel with your tongue, and lower your head until the water just covers your ears. Reach back and assure yourself that the tip of your snorkel is 8–10 cm (3–4 in.) above the surface. Now, remove your tongue from the mouthpiece and slowly breathe in.

Stay in position until you feel comfortable breathing. Look around and try swiveling your head to expand your range of vision. It's amazing how clearly you see with the mask! What you see is magnified, and in the shallow water, the brilliance of the sunlight is enhanced.

The float

When you feel comfortable with your snorkel, you can learn to float. Keeping your head submerged and the snorkel tip above water, put one hand down on the bottom. Inhale and fill your lungs with air. Slowly raise your knees off the bottom and straighten your back and legs. Your body will rise to the surface. As it does, spread your legs and straighten your back. Relax your muscles and let the water hold you up. Keeping one hand on the bottom as an anchor, you may want to reach the other arm out, to use as a balance. You are now floating on the surface with virtually no effort. This float is the basis for snorkeling. It will allow you to rest comfortably on the surface while examining the wonders below.

Breathing

It is necessary to keep a certain amount of air in your lungs in order to float. Until you are comfortable with the gear and have begun to swim about freely, try this: breathe in and out *slowly*, moving just enough air out of your lungs on each exhale to satisfy the feeling of needing to breathe. When you inhale, try to suck in more air, filling your lungs more than you would normally. You'll notice a resistance as you breathe, caused by the pressure of the water on your chest and by air resistance caused by using the snorkel. To overcome this slight pressure without effort, breathe from the diaphragm, the muscles in the upper stomach area that stretch and compress the lungs.

As you breathe in you'll float a little higher in the water and you'll sink slightly when you exhale.

Learning to float is easy if you take it one step at a time. From a crouching position on the bottom, straighten your legs while keeping one hand on the bottom for security. As you start to float to the surface, arch your back and spread arms and legs as far apart as is comfortable. You will bob to the surface, and once there, you can clear your snorkel and begin breathing. Keep as much air in your lungs as possible, and you will float higher in the water.

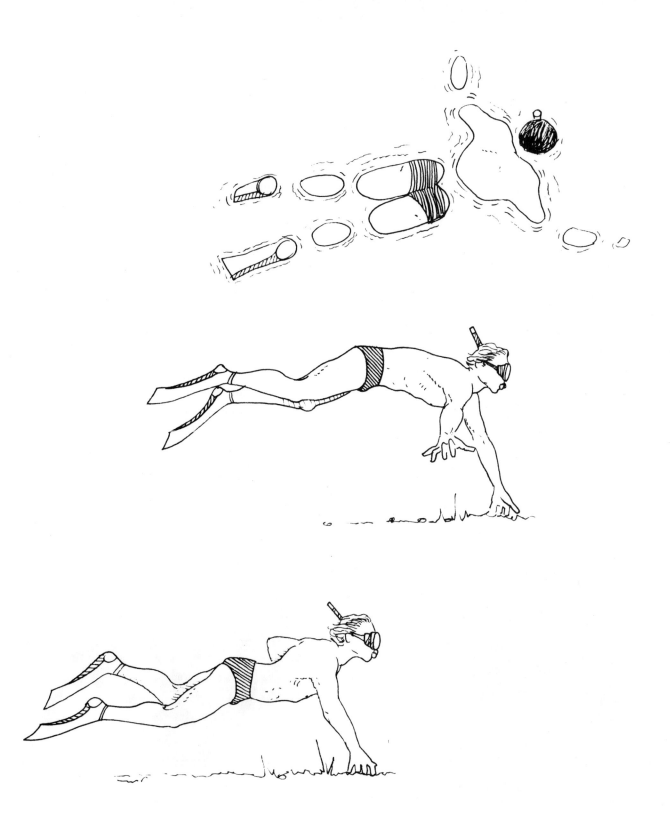

CLEARING THE MASK

If your mask fills with water while below the surface, it is very easy to clear while remaining under water. (Left) If your head is upright, with the top pointing toward the surface, simply press in on the top edge of the mask and blow gently. Air collecting in the top of the mask will force water out the bottom. (Right) If your head is not upright, turn so that one side of the mask is pointed at the surface and push in on side while blowing gently. Water will be forced out the side closest to the bottom.

While you were floating, a little water may have seeped into your mask. This is normal. Also, the glass faceplate may have fogged up. This, too, is normal. Both are easy to correct.

Kneeling in the water, take off your mask and rinse it. Spit into the mask and smear the saliva over the inside of the faceplate. Rinse the mask again. This will keep the glass from fogging. If you prefer, buy a bottle of mask-clearing fluid from a store that carries scuba diving equipment. This fluid must be used according to the instructions on the bottle. Spitting is simply more convenient and economical, and it is socially acceptable under the circumstances.

Put your mask on and position it firmly. Sitting down in the water, take a breath, close your air passages by blocking off the back of your throat with the back of your tongue, and duck your head under. Pull the top of the mask slightly away from your face, allowing water to seep in until the mask is about half full. Then straighten up so your head is above water and unblock the air passages. Take a deep breath, push in slightly on the top edge of the mask, and gently blow through your nose. The air from your nose will bubble up through the water, collect at the top of the mask, and force the water out the bottom edge. Remember to keep blowing

through your nose until the water is all out, or some water may creep up the nostrils.

An alternate method is to grasp the side of the mask with thumb at the bottom edge and fingers at the top, pull the bottom of the mask away from your face, and blow the water out.

Move out into slightly deeper water so that your head is submerged when you sit down and practice clearing your mask until you can do it while keeping your eyes open during the whole procedure.

Clearing while swimming

The procedures described above work best when your head is perpendicular to the surface, rather than parallel, as it will be when you are floating or swimming on the surface. To clear while swimming, stretch your neck out so that you are looking straight ahead, rather than down, and the bottom of the mask is parallel to the bottom of the water. Then take a deep breath, push in the top of the mask, and blow out as described earlier.

Another way to clear the mask while swimming is to roll your head sideways, push on the upper side of the mask, and blow. For example if you roll your head so that you are looking at your left shoulder, the left side of the mask will be closest to the surface. Push in on the left rim and exhale as before. The water will be forced out the right side, which will be parallel to the bottom.

To keep the faceplace from fogging while you are in the water, spit in the mask and smear the saliva over the inside of the glass, then rinse with water and put the mask on. Defogging solutions are also available.

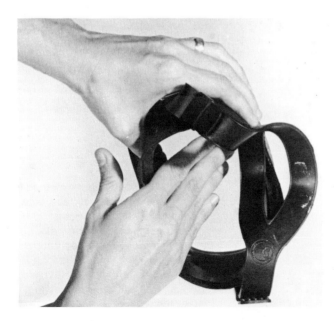

CLEARING THE SNORKEL

Even if you never dive below the surface, water—from a wave or from splashes—will find its way into your snorkel. The first time it happens you'll inhale a little and come up sputtering. Don't worry; it happens to everybody.

Kneel in shallow water with your mask and snorkel in place and put your face under water. Breathe in and out several times, then inhale, hold your breath, and plug the snorkel with your tongue. When water fills the snorkel, it may creep back in your mouth if not blocked. Keeping your tongue in the mouthpiece will also remind you not to breathe in until the snorkel has been cleared of water. Duck your head under until the snorkel is submerged and fills with water.

Now raise your head until your ears are level with the surface. Pull your tongue out of the mouthpiece, and, as you do, close your nostrils and blow sharply into the snorkel. The water will squirt out of the top.

Do not inhale deeply. There may be a little water left in the snorkel. To check, inhale very slowly. If there is water inside, it will gurgle as you inhale. Take in air, then blow hard and sharply again. This should completely clear the snorkel.

This is called the blast method of snorkel clearing; it takes a hard blast to clear the snorkel. A good way to avoid inhaling water is to not completely empty your lungs when you first blow to clear the snorkel; keep back enough air for the second blast.

In the blast clearing method, after you break surface, blow sharply into the snorkel mouthpiece, forcing water up and out the tip. Keep enough air back in your lungs for a second, shorter blow in case there is a little water left in the snorkel.

Displacement clearing

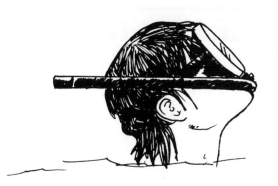

The blast method works well for both surface snorkelers and free divers. However, when free diving to 3–6 meters (10–20 ft.), you may want to try the displacement method to clear your snorkel. There are two advantages to this method–it does not take muscular effort to blow the water, and the snorkel is clear and ready to use as soon as you break surface.

To learn this method, stand in water that is at least chest deep. Breathe in and out several times, then inhale, hold your breath, and plug the snorkel mouthpiece with your tongue as before.

Now drop down under the water and push off forward and down. You should be able to stay close to the bottom by kicking slightly with your fins. When your chest is parallel to the bottom, look up to the surface and head up at an angle. As you do so, remove your tongue from the snorkel mouthpiece, and blow a small amount of air into the snorkel. Continue going up, keeping your head back so the tip of the snorkel points toward the bottom. As you break surface, the air you blew into the snorkel will push the water out. Any remaining water can be cleared with a short blast.

The key to getting all the water out is to keep the tip of the snorkel pointed down toward the bottom. By stretching your neck back and coming up at a slight angle, you'll find displacement clearing is easy.

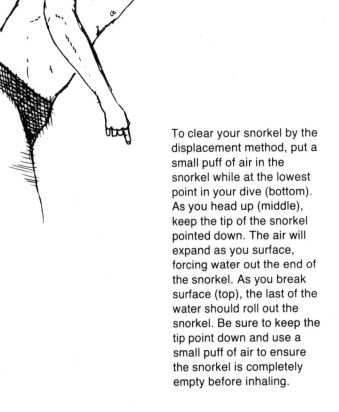

To clear your snorkel by the displacement method, put a small puff of air in the snorkel while at the lowest point in your dive (bottom). As you head up (middle), keep the tip of the snorkel pointed down. The air will expand as you surface, forcing water out the end of the snorkel. As you break surface (top), the last of the water should roll out the snorkel. Be sure to keep the tip point down and use a small puff of air to ensure the snorkel is completely empty before inhaling.

CLEARING THE EARS

Air in the inner ear is trapped and compresses or expands as the pressure on the eardrum increases or decreases. Water pressing on the eardrum increases pressure in the inner ear, compressing the air inside and causing the eardrum to bow inward. To compensate, when diving below the surface, you must "clear" the ear by introducing more air into the inner ear through the eustachian tube which connects with the throat.

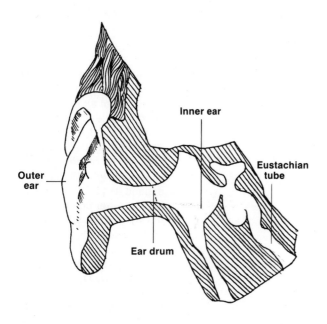

As you went down toward the bottom to practice displacement clearing, you probably noticed a feeling of pressure in your ears. Although you are not aware of it, at sea level, the weight of the air above you pushes down on your body with a force equal to 1 kilogram per square centimeter (4.7 lbs. per sq. in.). As you decrease the amount of air above you, by going up a mountain or to the top of a tall building, the pressure exerted by the air decreases. As you go down the mountain in a car or down a fast elevator, you may feel the air pressure increasing in your ears.

There a number of spaces within the body that are filled with air, notably the sinuses and the inner ear. As the pressure increases on the outside of your body, the air in these spaces is compressed—that is, its volume shrinks. The effect of this is to cause the eardrum (see diagram) to stretch as the outside pressure pushes the thin skin inward. To relieve the pressure, you must get enough air into the inner ear to push back against the inside of the eardrum with a force equal to the pressure outside. This process is called clearing the ears.

Fortunately, nature has provided a system of air passages and valves inside the head to do this. If you have driven a car down a tall mountain or flown in an airplane, you have probably felt pressure on your ears as you descended. At some point, your ears probably "popped"—that is, you heard a noise, a crack, and immediately the sensation of pressure disappeared. This pop was caused by air rushing into your inner ear from the eustachian tube as the pressure naturally equalized in your ear.

How to clear your ears

In a car, plane, or elevator, the pressure increases very gradually because of the great amount of air you must pass through to make a noticeable difference in pressure. Unless your air passages are clogged by a cold or allergy, the ears usually clear by themselves. In the water, however, you must take positive action to clear your ears even if you do not dive very far below the surface.

Some people, especially those with small eustachian tubes or chronic sinus problems, may have difficulty learning to clear. Once you've learned, it becomes much easier with practice. After a few sessions, you should be able to clear your ears quickly and almost effortlessly.

The key to easy ear clearing is to put air into the ear at the surface before you go down. As you go down, the pressure on the ear will cause the eustachian tube to collapse. If you wait to equalize until you feel the pressure, you will probably have some difficulty, because the tube that carries the air will have flattened out.

The eardrum and the parts of the inner ear affected by air pressure are delicate. It is important to clear gently—*never blow, sharply,* as you did when clearing the snorkel.

Just as a collapsed eustachian tube won't carry air, a stretched tube will carry air more easily. Standing at the surface, with mask in place, pinch your nostrils closed by placing a thumb and index finger into the finger pockets in the bottom of the mask and squeezing. Do not close off the pharynx (the nasal passages). Tilt your head as far to one side as you can. As your neck stretches, so does the eustachian tube. Now, gently, using only the muscles in your neck, blow into your nose. With the nose and mouth closed, there is only one place the air can go—into the eustachian tube and on to the ear. When you feel the outward pressure on your eardrum, stop blowing. The ear is cleared and should be equalized for dives to 4.5–6.0 meters (15–20 ft.). If you dive deeper, you will probably have to equalize again.

Now clear the other ear by tilting your head to the other side and repeating the procedure. To release the pressure inside the ears, simply swallow hard or yawn. This will open the eustachian tube and let the air out.

Practice until you can feel the eustachian tube working and can equalize at will. To equalize while swimming, instead of stretching toward the shoulder, turn the ear you wish to clear toward the surface, stretch the neck forward to pull the eustachian tube taut, and blow.

If you have trouble

If you have tried the technique described above and still can't clear, your sinuses are probably clogged. In this case, especially if you have a cold with sinus congestion, you may want to snorkel at the surface without diving down. If you still want to clear and dive, taking a non-prescription decongestant will probably clear the sinuses. Most nasal sprays are also effective. Antihistamines can make you sleepy, so read the labels on these preparations carefully, and follow directions. Stores that carry diving equipment may sell a mild antihistamine spray called Ear-Eze which will help clear the sinuses.

The key to easy ear clearing is to blow *gently* into the nose while pinching the nostrils shut. If you have trouble, try stretching your head to one side while blowing. This will pull on the eustachian tube and make it easier to clear the ear on that side.

KICKS

The fins make swimming while snorkeling almost
effortless, and they give you the power you need to
stay under while surface diving. To get the most
power from your kicks with the least effort, you do
not kick as you would were you swimming without
fins. Without fins, you kick from the knees down,
using the calf muscles to raise and lower the legs.
Fins, however, allow you to use the more powerful
thigh and buttock muscles, which do not tire as
quickly. Ordinarily, the hands are not used when
swimming with fins; let them trail at your sides or
clasp them behind your back.

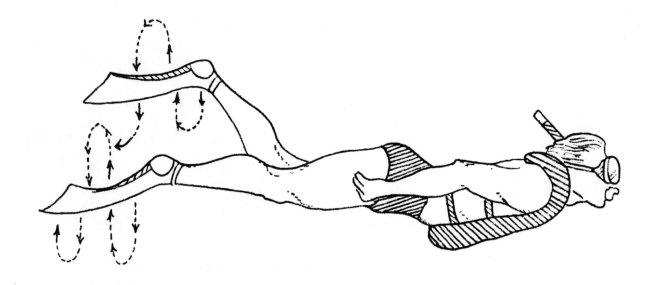

Flutter kick

The most commonly used kick, and the most powerful, is called the flutter kick. From the basic arms-out float, bring your arms down and keep them loosely at your sides. Hold your legs, particularly the knees, fairly stiff, with the feet side by side. Now begin rolling your hips slowly from side to side, using your thigh muscles to move the legs and fins up and down in a steady, smooth scissors motion (see illustration).

Keep the legs and knees straight, and let your buttocks, hips, and thighs do the work. With a slow, steady rhythm, you'll be able to swim long distances without tiring. The work of moving you through the water is done by the pushing action of the blades of the fins against the water. It is important to keep the fins in the water at all times. As when swimming without fins, kicking with the feet out of the water produces a lot of foam and splash and not much movement. Lifting the fins clear of the water actually takes a lot of effort; to really move, keep your legs straight, roll your hips, and keep your fins in the water.

The flutter kick is the simplest and one of the most efficient of all kicks using swim fins. While keeping the knees rigid and slightly bent, roll the hips and push with the thigh muscles. As one fin heads up, the other should be moving down. Do not push too hard; a slow, steady kick will get you farther with less effort than a rapid kick that tires you quickly.

Shuffle kick

The shuffle kick is similar to the flutter. Straighten your legs and keep them straight. Place one foot directly on top of the other. Move your legs apart quickly; one straight up and the other down. Now move the legs back together, coming to rest one atop the other.

Hands

To keep your body streamlined and present the least resistance to the water, it is best to let the arms trail loosely by your sides. Occasionally you may want to use your hands to treat water over one spot, to balance in rough water, or to help get under during a surface dive.

Frog kick

Once in a while, to rest your legs and thighs, you may want to switch to the frog kick. This uses a different set of muscles and is an excellent change of pace.

With your arms by your sides, bend your knees outward and draw your feet together with the soles touching (see diagram). Kick out, moving each fin in a semi-circle as you straighten your legs; then draw your legs straight together behind you, and glide. Then bend your knees, draw your legs together and repeat. After each kick, glide a few seconds to rest your legs.

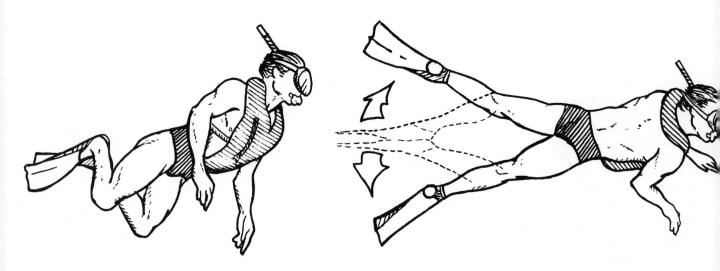

Releasing cramps

If you take things smoothly and easily, you should not encounter any difficulties. However, at some point you may experience a cramp—a painful spasm in a muscle. If you are wearing open-heel fins, you may get a cramp in the instep or arch of your foot until you get used to the fins.

Releasing a cramp in the water is simple. If the cramp is in the front of the leg, reach back, grab the ankle of the cramped leg, and pull the leg up and back. If the cramp is in the back of the leg, or in the instep of the foot, reach forward, grasp the tip of the fin, and pull until the cramp releases.

Cramps are one of the reasons you should snorkel with a buddy. If the methods above don't release a cramp, your buddy can swim over and massage the muscle vigorously.

Avoiding cramps

The best way to deal with cramps is to avoid them. Don't overtax any set of muscles. If your thighs feel tired, float a while and rest them, then change to another style of kick. In some cases, cramps can be aggravated by a deficiency of potassium in your diet (see page 65 for other effects of potassium deficiency). Before entering the water, drink an electrolyte-replacement fluid such as Gatorade, take potassium tablets, or eat potassium-rich foods such as bananas.

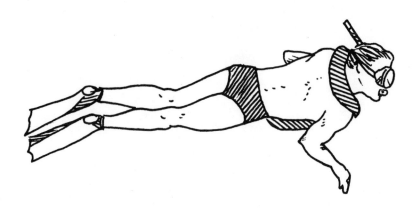

The frog kick is an excellent change of pace from the flutter kick, as it uses a completely different set of muscles. Reading the drawing from left to right, the first position is the beginning of each stroke. From a floating position, draw your legs down and outward until the knees are distended and the bottoms of the fins are touching each other. The middle position is the power part of the stroke: from the first position, straighten your knees and kick the fins outward forcefully. The third position is the glide part of the stroke: after kicking out, draw your legs back together while your body glides forward, then get ready to return to the first position.

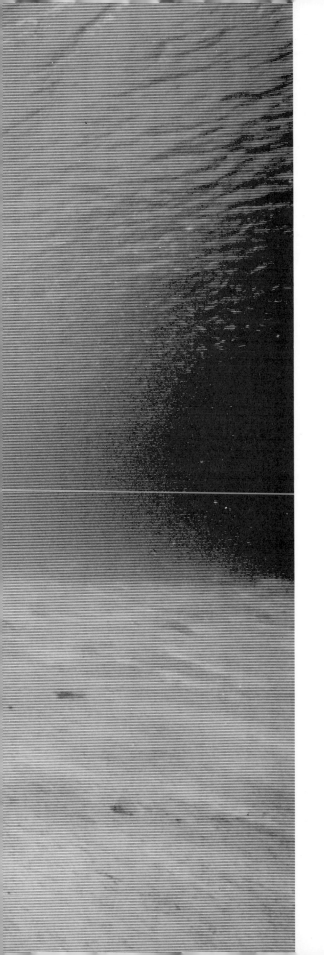

4 | The pike dive
The slant dive

Surface
Diving

THE PIKE DIVE

By now you've experimented with swimming under the water as well as on top. The difficulty in free diving is not in staying afloat, but in fighting your body's natural buoyancy in order to stay under. Especially in salt water, with lungs full of air, the average person tends to pop up to the surface.

One way to counteract this buoyancy is to exhale slightly, reducing the volume of air in the lungs, before diving under. This obviously shortens the length of time you'll be able to stay under before coming up.

Another way is to carry some lead weights with you. This involves a more advanced type of diving. The technique is covered in Chapter 7.

The most convenient way to free dive is to make a pike dive from the surface. This uses your body weight to push you toward the bottom. Once submerged, you can stay down as long as you can hold your breath, by swimming forward, and keeping your face down or straight ahead. Essentially, you are using your body as an air foil to produce negative lift (downward pressure). The water pressure on your back counteracts your natural buoyancy and helps keep you down with minimum effort. When ready to surface, you simply look up. Now the forward motion creates water pressure on your chest, which, with your buoyancy, pushes you easily to the surface.

The accompanying illustrations show the steps in a complete free dive. The pike dive can be executed while floating, but, especially, in the beginning, it may be easier to try while swimming forward.

Before the start of each dive, you must remember to *clear your ears at the surface*. This will conserve air for your dive and prevent any discomfort on the way down. If you can't clear, *don't dive*.

The pike dive is the most popular way to get under water from a floating position on the surface. The dive does not end when you are under water, however; as described in the text, the second half of the dive — the ascent — is just as important as the beginning.

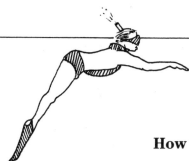 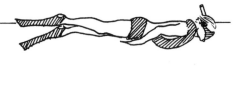

How to do it

From the surface, while swimming forward, take in a breath and bend sharply forward at the waist. Your head should be pointed nearly straight down. When your body is at a 90-degree angle to the surface, pop your legs up in the air, as nearly perpendicular to the water's surface as possible. The weight of your legs, unsupported in the air, will cause you to sink toward the bottom. Use your hands as in a breast stroke to move yourself toward and down. When you feel your fins below the surface, kick hard.

Level off. You will now be headed down. When you have reached the depth you desire, level off, while continuing to kick with your fins. As long as you keep swimming forward, you will stay under.

Turn Up. When you feel the urge to breathe, look up and continue kicking. You will immediately begin to ascend. Since you don't know what may be above you on the surface, keep your eyes open and head tilted back, looking straight up. Straighten one arm above your head, with the hand in a fist. Slowly spiral in a full circle while ascending, watching the surface carefully for rocks, piers, boats, or other floating objects as you come up. The spiraling action compensates for the decreased field of vision caused by the mask by helping you check the areas slightly ahead, behind, and to both sides of the spot where you'll be surfacing.

Surface. When your head breaks surface you will "breach," or pop up slightly above the water. As your body drops back to the surface, clear your snorkel. Remember, *do not inhale sharply* until you are sure there is no water left in the barrel.

THE SLANT DIVE

An alternative to the pike drive is the slant, or headfirst, dive. Like the pike dive, it is started by swimming forward with the mask in the water. You increase speed by finning harder. Once you duck your head under, water pressure on your back will cause you to head down while moving forward. You must keep up the vigorous finning and keep your head down, or your natural buoyancy will cause you to pop up to the surface. The more sharply you duck your head, the more quickly you'll go under.

The main advantages of the headfirst dive is that it is easier to execute than the pike. The disadvantages are that it takes more effort to get under this way because you are using muscles instead of body weight to counteract natural buoyancy, and you will not be able to dive as deeply using this method.

Rest

After each short excursion under water, you should rest by floating on the surface or swimming forward slowly for one or two minutes. Although you may not feel tired, this interval allows the level of oxygen in your blood to "catch up" and return to normal. Contrary to popular belief, it is *not* the lack of oxygen in your lungs that is the primary cause of the urge to breathe. It is, instead, the presence of carbon dioxide, the by-product of respiration, that stimulates breathing.

When periodically holding your breath, as when you free dive, it is possible to lower the amount of oxygen in the blood without feeling the need to breathe. This is why it is important to rest a minute at the surface, inhaling and exhaling deeply to avoid accidentally lowering your oxygen level.

A float

Particularly if you are in an area frequented by boaters, you may want to tow a small float with the red-and-white diver's flag on it. This will warn boaters of your presence. The float can also be used to rest on between dives, and is an excellent safety accessory (see page 64).

For safe, enjoyable snorkeling, it is important not to exhaust yourself. Rest between dives and always try to move with the currents and surges rather than against them.

Safety Tips

- Never begin a dive when you are breathing heavily or feel winded. Wail until your breathing is normal.
- Before diving, breathe deeply through the snorkel.
- Until you've mastered the technique of pike diving, it may help to exhale slightly before starting the dive to reduce your buoyancy.
- Remember to plug the snorkel mouthpiece with your tongue to keep water out of your mouth.
- Get your legs up quickly, and as straight as possible.
- Use your hands if needed to help pull yourself under.
- Kick hard with the fins as soon as the blades are in the water.
- When you feel the urge to breathe, start up *immediately.*
- Do not try to go ''just a little farther''; you'll only tire yourself needlessly and may induce hypoxia.
- On the way up, extend one arm in front as a bumper.
- Look up!
- Turn slowly in a complete circle to ensure there is nothing above.
- Listen for boats.
- Blow sharply to clear the snorkel.
- Do not inhale deeply until you are sure the snorkel is clear.
- Rest two minutes before diving again.

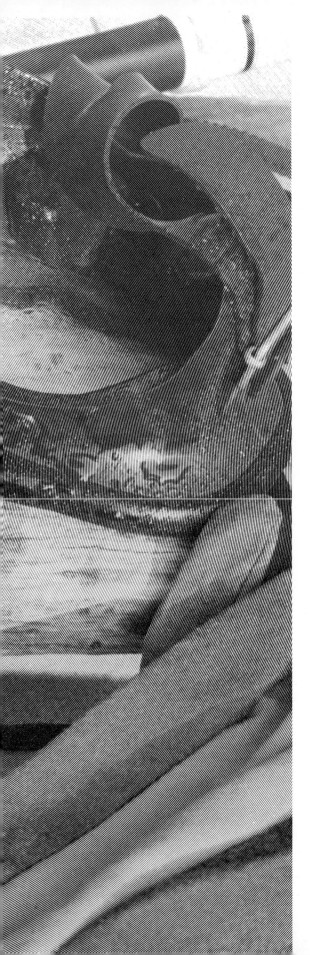

5 | **Be safe**
**Marine life to
    watch out for**

Water
Safety

BE SAFE

It is easy to be safe in the water if you use common sense and follow a few basic rules. The first, common to all water activities, is to buddy up. Pair up with a friend. Being a swim or snorkel buddy means being close enough—and aware enough—at all times to be able to help your partner. It's more fun to share the experience, and you can't do that if you're too far away to help your buddy.

Sun

The most common discomfort snorkelers encounter is sunburn. Your body may feel cool as you snorkel because you'll be covered by water. Your skin, however, will receive a heavy dose of ultraviolet light, the kind that produces sunburn.

You'll be floating on your stomach, looking down most of the time, so the most vulnerable areas are your back and the back of your neck, arms, knees, and legs. If you don't plan to wear a wet suit (see pp.100–101), wear a shirt, preferably a long-sleeved one to protect your back and arms. You might also want to wear a pair of lightweight trousers or jeans to protect your legs. Ordinary suntan lotion washes off quickly, so wear a waterproof sun-screening lotion, such as zinc oxide ointment, on the back of your neck and behind your knees.

It's easy to get hooked on snorkeling and to forget how long you've been out. Stop occasionally and check exposed skin for redness. Push in on the skin and let go quickly. If the spot you pushed on looks very white compared to the surrounding area, you're on your way to a burn. Take it easy and build up a tan before going on a marathon snorkeling binge.

A float and a flag

If you're snorkeling in an area with motorboat traffic, you must have a diving flag with you. In the United States and the Caribbean, the dive flag is bright red with a diagonal white stripe. In other areas, the international ships' flag "A" means "divers down, stay clear." Dive flags on poles with styrofoam floats are cheap and available at any store that sells scuba diving equipment. Attach 9–12 meters (30–40 ft.) of nylon rope to the float, tie a loop in one end, and hold this loop in your hand as you snorkel. The float will follow you as you move around.

A useful accessory for extended snorkeling trips, and a convenient place for the flag, is a diver's float made out of a tire inner tube with a piece of 6 mm (¼ in.) marine plywood on top. You can use this float to rest on or to hold shells while shelling. You may want to tow the float, or better, attach the float to a small anchor with about 12 meters (40 feet) of rope. Anchor the float, snorkel around, then just pull up the anchor and put it on top of the float while you move to another location.

Safety starts at home

Water safety starts at home, before you go snorkeling. Take out the telephone book or call an operator and request the numbers of a law enforcement office, an air-sea rescue or ambulance service, and the closest doctor or hospital. Write these numbers on a card and put it in something you'll be carrying with you.

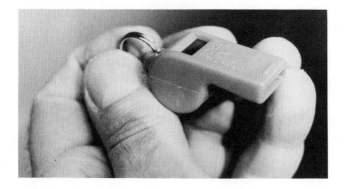

A whistle can be a great aid in signaling for someone's attention. If you get caught in a strong current or are in need of assistance, it can be a real lifesaver.

Eat right

It's important to eat right before any physical activity. You'll need a proper breakfast. Any of these are good: Eggs (not fried), toast, jelly, pancakes, sweet rolls, waffles, and juice. Milk may be difficult to digest or may sour in your stomach with the sun and exertion. Greasy food, too, are hard to digest and may not go well with the exercise and the inevitable rise and fall of the water. Coffee and tea contribute to the faster elimination of body fluids. On a hot day, this could push you toward dehydration.

A light meal high in carbohydrates found in foods such as breads, cereal, fruit, and vegetables is ideal before snorkeling. If you eat a heavier meal, wait several hours before entering the water. This will allow your body time to absorb the nutrients.

Of the many minerals you need in your daily diet, potassium is the most critical when you snorkel. Potassium is used by the muscles in the conversion of body sugars to energy. A depletion of potassium can lead to exhaustion and muscle cramps and even, in extreme cases, to heart attack. Eating foods such as bananas, oranges, and dried fruit will prevent a potassium shortage as will drinking electrolyte-replacement beverages such as Gatorade.

Calcium and magnesium are also important to good muscle function. A depletion of either can lead to muscle cramps and spasms, or to chronic fatigue. Calcium can be obtained from milk or cheese. Magnesium is found in plant foods such as wheat or nuts.

A high-calorie, nutrient-rich food to take with you if you plan an extended outing is called "gorp." A general recipe is: One box of granola cereal, 200 grams (7 ounces) of peanuts, 200 grams of cashews or other nuts, one large box (about 0.5 kilograms or 1 pound) raisins and 225 grams (about ½ pound) or M&M's or similar small chocolate candies.

When snorkeling, a float with a divers' flag attached will warn boaters away from you. In many areas, a float and flag are required by law. The flag above is recognized by sport divers throughout the United States and in many places around the world. It means "Stay away, divers down." The flag below is the internationally recognized symbol for "diver down," also known as the "A" or Alpha Flag.

MARINE LIFE TO WATCH OUT FOR

Sea Urchin. These creatures are common on most coral reefs. Encounters with them can be painful, but they are easily avoided.

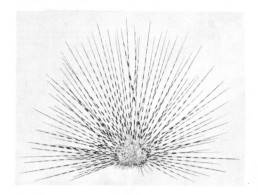

Portuguese Man-o'-War. Stings from this animal can be quite painful, but they are not very common.

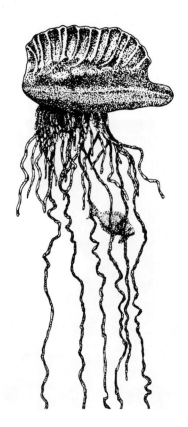

Just as in a jungle or a forest, once you're in the water, you'll have to respect the other creatures around you. Most are totally harmless, but there are a few precautions you should take.

Rays. There are many species of rays. Some of these have a barbed stinger at the end of their tails which they use to stun their prey. Rays sometimes lie on the bottom and cover themselves with sand. Shuffle your feet when walking in the water, and avoid scraping your body against the bottom when free diving.

Urchins. Sea urchins are a far more common nuisance. Look at the bottom as you enter the water. If you see urchins, be careful to step around them. The urchins' spines are very sharp, like needles. If you brush up against one, the spines will puncture the skin and break off inside. The spines burn, and the area around them may swell. General treatment for urchin spines is to pull out as many as you can with tweezers, then rub a meat-tenderizing powder (papain is the active ingredient) or hydrocortisone cream on the area.

Jellyfish. Jellyfish are colonies of small animals. They may be small or large, and they look like clear or milky blobs of gelatin. If you encounter large numbers of jellyfish, leave the water. Brushing against one will cause a mild burning sensation. Wash the affected area, and rub on meat tenderizer or hydrocortisone cream.

Man o' war. The Portuguese man o' war is related to the jellyfish. It has a large, triangular, gas-filled float, below which are streamers of stinging cells. These streamers can be 1.25 meters (4 ft.) in length. Contact with a man o' war's tentacles will cause severe burning almost immediately. The man o' war, although known in all ocean areas around the United States and the Caribbean, is not all that common. Anyone stung by a man o' war should leave or be taken from the water immediately. If any tentacles are still clinging to skin, remove them with a tweezer or similar object; be careful not to touch them yourself. Get the victim to a doctor immediately.

Fire coral. Fire coral is a mustard-colored animal that looks like coral, but is actually related to the jellyfish. If you brush against it, you'll feel as though you've been stung by a jellyfish. Meat tenderizer or hydrocortisone cream is the best treatment.

Coral. Coral is not a plant, but actually a colony of small animals. The hard part of the coral is composed of skeletons of these animals that have died. Only the outermost layer of the coral is alive. Some corals secrete an enzyme that can irritate the skin. If you scrape yourself against a coral, it may cut and leave the enzyme behind. Hydrocortisone cream will ease the discomfort.

Use common sense. Common-sense precautions will protect you in the water just as they do on land. Look arouond and see what kind of creatures are near you. Don't scrape the bottom or coral formations. Don't stick your hand under anything or into a hole. Something unpleasant, such as a moray eel, may be there.

Sting Ray. Carefully watching where you step is the best method to avoid these creatures. The stingers must be removed surgically, and can cause considerable pain.

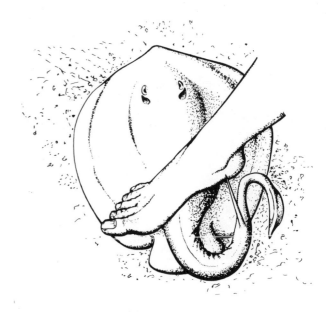

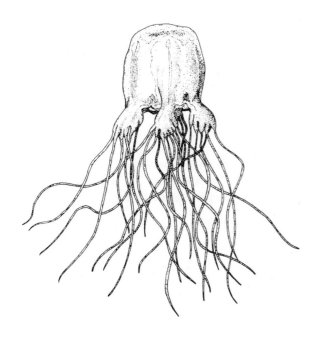

Box Jellyfish. Though most jellyfish are not truly dangerous, the box jellyfish is. In Australia, where they are frequently found, they are considered deadly. They are occasionally seen in the Caribbean, although the variety there, while carefully regarded, is not considered a killer.

Other concerns

Sharks. The danger to humans from sharks is overstated. All the oceans and even some rivers, have sharks. (Upland forests have bears, cougars, and snakes.) Observe the area in which you intend to snorkel and ask some people familiar with the area if it is especially known for shark sightings. Avoid areas under or around fishing piers, fish canneries, or processing areas. If you wander into an area where you think there may be sharks, or if you spot a shark, avoid splashing unnecessarily. As quietly as possible, swim to shore. Most sharks avoid humans. Known exceptions to this rule are the Pacific gray reef shark, the great white shark, and the hammerhead and blue sharks. If any of these species are especially plentiful in your intended snorkeling area, find a new spot.

Barracudas. The barracuda is a fearsome-looking fish—fast, torpedo-shaped, and seemingly all teeth. Barracudas are not normally dangerous to people. There have been a very few reports of barracudas attacking swimmers in the Pacific, and any barracuda over 1.25 meters (4 ft.) long should be considered potentially dangerous. Avoid wearing shiny jewelry or other bright objects while snorkeling around barracudas.

Scorpion fish. One other fish, common to a degree in all ocean areas, is the scorpion fish. The various species—sculpins, stonefish, lion fish, zebra fish—found in the Pacific and Indian oceans, are deadly. These fish have a powerful poison which is injected when a person steps on or bumps the fish. Most types of scorpion fish inject the poison through a special dorsal fin (on top of the body).

Stonefish sometimes lie on the bottom of a reef. Since they look very much like rocks, they are a little hard to spot. Do not walk on coral or rock reefs barefoot, and don't scrape against the bottom when free diving. If you are stung, get back to the beach, tell someone you've been stung, and get to a hospital immediately.

Scorpion fish and their relatives should be left alone and their beauty enjoyed from a safe distance. They are not known to be aggressive, but may sting if touched.

Barracudas have a bad reputation, but they pose no threat to prudent snorkelers.

Barnacles. Barnacles are crustaceans that attach themselves in colonies to stationary objects—rocks, wrecks, pilings, and so forth. Try to avoid brushing against them, as their sharp edges can inflict cuts and abrasions. Treat barnacle cuts as you would treat any cut from a sharp object.

Moray eels. These shy creatures have received a bad reputation, probably because they bear some resemblance to snakes. However, if provoked, they can give a nasty wound. Morays live in crevasses in rocks and coral formations and catch their food by striking out at passing fish from the shelter of their caves. To avoid a moray bite, keep your hands out of holes and crevasses and don't hand feed them. The bite of a moray is not venomous, but rotting food particles in its mouth can cause a serious infection if the wound is not properly treated. Medical attention should be sought for moray bites.

On certain occasions, morays leave their holes and swim free but they do not pursue and attack their prey at this time. Should you be approached by a free-swimming moray, remain still until it goes away—which won't take long. It is best to observe these graceful and fascinating creatures—from a respectful distance.

Barnacles pose one of the greatest threats to snorkelers, especially when exiting the water near slippery rocks.

Moray eels have also gained a bad reputation, but in fact they are not dangerous when left alone.

6 | **Shelling**
Fish feeding
Marine studies
Photography

Snorkeling
Activities

SHELLING

Once you have practiced the various skills a few times, you should be a competent snorkeler. Many people are perfectly content to stop there, getting great pleasure from paddling about on the surface or making an occasional surface dive. Others see the basic skills as just a way to get around in the water. There are a number of activities to involve you once you've learned the basics. Sightseeing, shelling, lobstering, diving for abalone, fish feeding, and underwater photography are among them.

Of course, you'll be sightseeing any time you're in the water with a mask, but learning a little bit about water and shore environments will make the experience much more enjoyable. There are a number of books describing the various underwater environments and the life forms that inhabit them.

When you know something about the different types of underwater settings, you may want to try snorkeling in each. A shallow ocean reef area and a fresh-water river are very different experiences. There are literally thousands of different sea shells, each the home of a different type of mollusk. These range from the giant tridacna clams of the South Pacific down to tiny periwinkles hardly larger than a pencil eraser. While some shells are drab, and unin-teresting, many are fantastically shaped or brilliantly colored and patterned with stripes, rings, or dots.

Shells are found in most ocean areas, but larger and brighter shells are most abundant in the tropics.

Look for shells on the bottom around tropical reefs or in strands of eel grass (a marine plant that resembles border grass). When diving in an area covered with eel grass, look carefully before you reach, as other creatures, such as crabs or scorpion fish, could be in there as well.

Be aware, too, that many of the shells you pick up will have an animal living inside. Take your shell to the surface, turn it over, and look inside. If the shell is alive, return it to the bottom. *Collect only empty shells.* If you collect a live shell, the animal inside will die soon after being taken from the water. Shortly thereafter, the shell will begin to smell very unpleasant. Only shells that are empty are safe to keep, and these should be dried for several days before being packed in a suitcase or other enclosed areas. Thick shells that have no thin partitions or fragile pieces can be boiled in water to help clean them. Collecting live animals is cruel. In many areas, it is also illegal.

If you are shelling in the Pacific, be sure you know what a cone shell looks like and avoid it. The animal that lives inside has a small barb which can inject a powerful poison.

This is just a small sampling of the wide variety of shells that a snorkeler can collect. Observe good conservation practices when shell collecting and read up on dangerous shells when collecting in the Pacific Ocean.

Among the most popular snorkeling activities are shelling and fish-feeding. (Right) A seashell is the home of a soft animal known as a mollusk. One of the most easily recognized is the Queen conch (pronounced "konk"). The shells shown here are empty, piled in the wake of a conch fisherman. Conch is a delicacy in the Caribbean and heavy commercial fishing has made the animals scarce throughout much of their range. Never remove any live (occupied) shell from the water. (Below) Fish-feeding is an easy way to attract a wide variety of beautifully colored fish into easy range for viewing and photographing. When you go out snorkeling, take along some table scraps in a plastic bag. When you come to a likely spot, start doling out bits from the bag — the fish will find you in no time. Some fish are particularly aggressive feeders and may even nibble at your fingers (you might want to wear gloves). The fish will stay with you until you run out of food or close up the bag.

FISH IDENTIFICATION

Queen angel

Rock beauty

Lizardfish

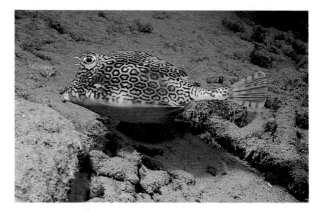

Cowfish

Grunt

French angel

Among the most beautiful and commonly seen reef fish are those illustrated in these pages. Not all are seen in all parts of the world, but wherever you dive or snorkel in tropical waters, you will see fish similar to these.

Hogfish

Rainbow parrotfish

Tang (juvenile)

Nassau grouper

French-striped grunt

Squirrelfish (with cleaner fish)

(Left) Fire coral is recognizable by its yellowish-brown color. While the shape shown here is the one most commonly seen, polyps may also attach themselves to other, normally harmless varieties of coral. Avoid brushing against fire coral, which can cause an unpleasant stinging sensation that may last for several days. (Below) A single coral head may exhibit a number of different types of corals and sponges. The long, tubular growths are tube sponges. The flat, rounded growth at lower left is brain coral. The mushroomlike formation in the upper right-hand corner is another frequently seen form. (Facing page) Puffer fish look fearsome, but they are shy and not particularly dangerous. When alarmed, they inflate themselves into balls, causing the long spines on their sides to stick straight out. Most predators will then avoid further contact with them.

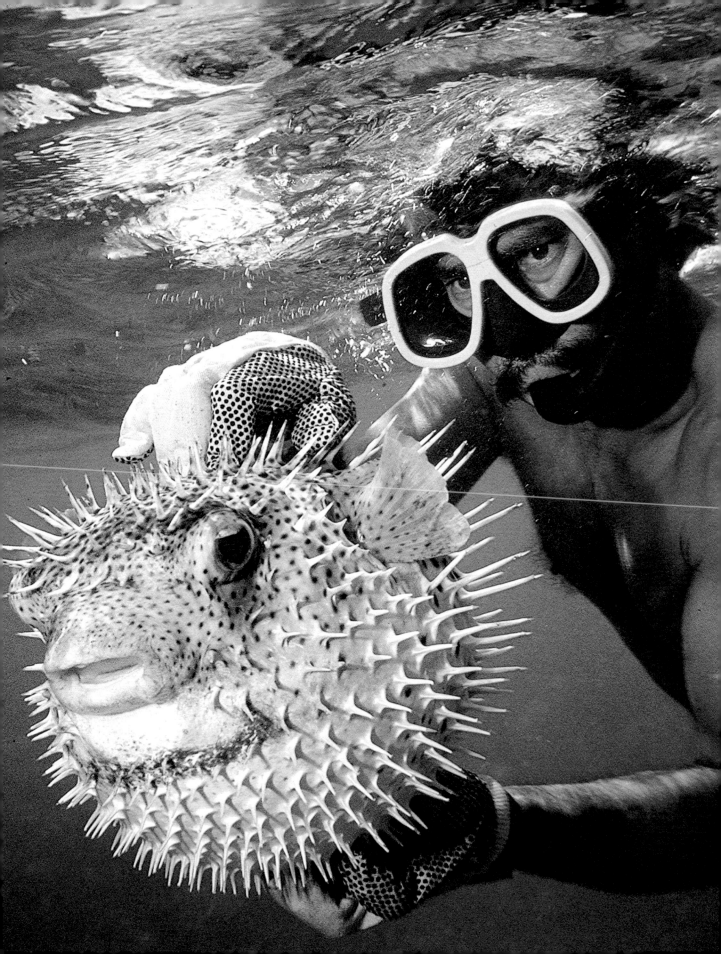

(Below) This photograph shows Atlantic spotted dolphins *(Stenella plagiodon)* playing tag with a snorkeler. Although many instances have been recorded of wild bottlenose dolphins *(Tursiops truncatus)* playing with humans, spotted dolphins live in the open ocean and seldom come into contact with man. These dolphins are part of a school being studied by Rick O'feldman, trainer of the bottlenose dolphin Flipper (of the TV series by that name). These Stenella dolphins are the only school of their type known to have permitted sustained observation by humans. The school is regularly seen in a shallow area of open ocean on the Bahama Bank. O'feldman attracts the dolphins by playing music into the water through underwater loudspeakers. Dolphins and whales are warm-blooded, air-breathing mammals, like man. They are keenly intelligent and communicate with each other using high-pitched squeals and whistles. (Facing page) Fresh-water areas are also excellent for diving and snorkeling. In Florida's Crystal River, and in other tropical and subtropical fresh-water areas in North and South America, live the gentle, homely manatee (often called sea-cows). Measuring between 3 and 4 meters (9–13 ft.) in length, these herbivorous aquatic mammals are harmless and curious.

(Right) Coral identification can become a lifetime passion. One of the most impressive types of branching coral is called elkhorn coral because of its resemblance to the horns of the North American elk. The colonies can grow into arrays 3–3.5 meters (10–12 ft.) in diameter. (Below) A snorkeler uses a Minolta Weathermatic to photograph a brain coral. Brain corals grow into a huge, boulderlike colonies, each with its own pattern of distinctive whorls.

FISH FEEDING

Just about anywhere you snorkel, there will be plenty of small fish around. Fish will eat almost anything, and spreading food in the water on a reef will attract a cloud of stunningly colored fish. Bread, cheese, or breakfast scraps will do fine. Before entering the water, put the food in a plastic bag. When you reach a likely area, open the bag and take a bit out. Close the bag tightly or you'll soon have more aggressive fish inside the bag eating all the food. You will notice a definite pecking order of fish species. Some will come right up to your face to get food, while others hang back and wait for scraps to float out to them. In the ocean, quite large fish can be attracted this way. The thrill of feeding a three-foot grouper is indescribable!

Fish feeding is a never-to-be-forgotten experience—especially for a child. It is a good idea to wear gloves when the more voracious feeders move in. Sergeant majors shown here are fairly gentle.

MARINE STUDIES

Corals and Anemones

Corals are the animals that form the beautiful, brightly colored structures and featherlike plumes of tropical reefs. The coral animals live in large groups, or colonies. Hard corals secrete limestone, and when they die, the limestone remains behind. Another coral animal will eventually build on top of this limestone skeleton, adding another layer of coral to the reef. This building process is very slow, and some types of coral grow less than a centimeter each year. A large colony of elkhorn coral may be a hundred years old.

Hard corals. Hard corals grow in many fantastic shapes, each shape according to species. Brain coral grows into large boulders, the wavy ridges on its surface reminiscent of the convoluted surface of a brain. Staghorn coral grows in large clumps that look like deer antlers. Plate coral grows in large, round sheets. Tabletop coral produces huge, umbrella-like structures which may be more than 2 meters (6 ft.) in diameter.

When snorkeling near coral, be careful not to bump into the colonies. The branching corals, in particular, may break off, killing a decade of growth and damaging the beauty of the reef. Also, though their structures may be fragile, underneath the thin layer of living tissue hard corals are sharp enough to slice your skin like a cheese grater.

Hard corals live in all oceans, in temperate, polar, and tropical seas. In the tropics, the corals gather in huge banks or reefs that may be kilometers long. Many species of coral live together on the reef, and together they form an oasis of life in the sea. Small fish, attracted by the algae and other food that grows on and around the reef, hide in the nooks and crannies from the larger fish that feed on them. Octopuses like the secluded holes in the reefs, as do eels and lobsters. Like a waterhole on the dry African plains, the reef is the focal point of activity, attracting every kind of ocean animal.

Reefs are usually marked on marine charts. They may be covered by only centimeters of water or they

The trumpetfish is attempting to look like the branches of soft coral on the left. Camouflage, which also includes color change, is its best method of defense. The background of the picture shows some of the various kinds of coral that can commonly be seen in tropical waters.

may start 30 meters (100 ft.) below the surface. Coral patches can be easily located by viewing the water from a bluff or the air. Reefs will show up as dark splotches or long, dark streaks in the lighter blue of the water.

Gorgonians and other soft corals. In addition to the rocky reef structure itself, corals are also responsible for many of its most valuable decorations. Soft corals—gorgonians, sea whips, sea fans—assume many flower or plant-like shapes. Sea fans are corals that branch into large, colorful structures. Sea feathers are large, bushy corals that look something like willow trees. Sea whips are fuzzy, many-armed colonies whose branches resemble the blossoms of a bottlebrush tree.

These various soft corals give the reef the atmosphere of a fairy garden: pinnacles and spires covered with strange flowers of fantastic coloration.

Anemones. Anemones are animals which, like corals, appear to be plants. The anemone has a number of long, colored tentacles surrounding a central mouth. It eats by drawing small fish down into the mouth with its tentacles. In cold water, anemones are often brightly colored—green, red, orange, or white—and may grow as large as a dinner plate. In the Pacific, a small, orange-striped fish, the clown fish, may live among the anemone's tentacles.

Field guides for snorkelers

A number of illustrated guides are available for snorkelers and divers interested in identifying and learning more about the fish and other marine life they encounter. Since these books may not be readily available at your hometown bookstores, we have listed their distributors. Many of these publications may be available at local dive shops.

Field Guide to the Atlantic Seashore from the Bay of Fundy to Cape Hatteras, by Kenneth L. Gosner, is a compact, comprehensive volume that illustrates just about every sea animal or plant you are likely to encounter in this area—except for fishes. Positive identifications are made through a combination of text descriptions and the excellent drawings and paintings. Closely related species are differentiated by detailed drawings that clearly point out the differences. The book covers over 900 species of invertebrates and 140 species of seaweeds, and also provides information on collecting and

preserving and on maintaining living specimens. Available through: Houghton Mifflin Co., 2 Park St., Boston, MA 02107.

Fishwatcher's Guide to West Atlantic Coral Reefs, by Charles C.G. Chaplin and illustrated by Peter Scott, was the first field guide designed for use underwater. It is printed on plastic pages and illustrates, in color, over 180 species of fishes. Similar species are presented together, with descriptions opposite each illustration. Available through: Harrowood Books, P.O. Box 397, Valley Forge, PA 19481.

Waterproof Guide to Corals & Fishes of Florida, the Bahamas and the Caribbean, by Idaz and Jerry Greenberg, is also produced to be used underwater without fear of it falling apart. The book contains color illustrations of 260 organisms, including 42 species of corals and 185 fishes. A few turtles and miscellaneous common invertebrates are also included. Identification is simplified by placing similar species next to each other and by providing a

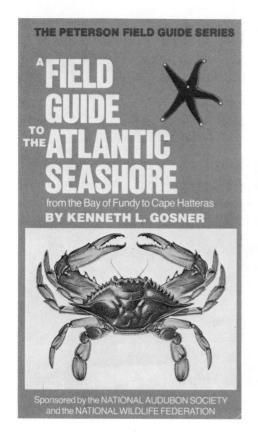

brief description opposite each creature. Available through: Seahawk Press, 6840 S.W. 92 St., Miami, FL 33156.

Also by the Greenbergs, and available through the same source, are a pair of plastic cards—one illustrating fish, the other common invertebrates (including corals)—that can be taken into the waters of the Caribbean instead of the book. The cards are printed on both sides and use the same illustrations as the Greenbergs' book, although by necessity not all of them.

Plastic cards are also available from Sea Sports, illustrating fishes of different areas: Florida and the Caribbean, the U.S. West Coast, Hawaii and the Central Pacific, and the Northeastern U.S. A separate card shows common invertebrates found at the shoreline and reef. Available through: Sea Sports, 10 Buckingham Pl., Norwalk, CT 06851.

The *Handbook of Hawaiian Fishes*, by William Gosline and Vernon Brock, provides the last word in the identification of the fishes of this region. Written with the serious layperson in mind, considerable information is provided on biology and ecology, including aspects of Hawaiian marine ecology, fish evolution, and anatomical features useful in differentiating one fish from another. Identification depends on a series of descriptive keys, first at the family level and then to genera and species. The keys require a certain level of technical expertise. The key to families has outline drawings to accompany the text, making identification, at least on this level, quite easy. Available through: The University Press of Hawaii, 2840 Kolowalu St., Honolulu, HI 96822.

Field Guide to the Coral Reefs of Florida and the Caribbean, by Eugene H. Kaplan, packs large amounts of information into a pocket-size book. Written for the layperson, the book describes common organisms, beginning at the seashore and moving deeper and deeper into the sea. Emphasis on ecology is as strong as on identification. The book is divided into two sections, the first describing each habitat (intertidal zone, turtle-grass beds, fringing and bank/barrier coral reefs, mangrove swamps), the second giving full descriptions of each marine species most likely to be found in the Caribbean and southern Florida. There are color underwater photographs of fishes which, together with descriptions, cover about 100 species. Available through: Houghton Mifflin Co., 2 Park St., Boston, MA 02107.

The *Fishwatcher's Guide to the Inshore Fishes of the Pacific Coast*, by Daniel W. Gotshall, is a colorful guide to 93 of the shallow-water fishes of the Pacific Coast. The book consists of brief descriptions, often with notes on differentiating similar species, and large color photographs of excellent quality. A

key in the first few pages makes it possible to identify a fish to the family level, providing both technical information and small drawings. Because the book does not go into great detail on fish ecology and anatomy, you might want to use this in conjunction with a more technical book. A companion volume, *Pacific Coast Subtidal Marine Invertebrates: A Fishwatcher's Guide,* by Gotshall and Laurence L. Laurent, takes a somewhat more extensive look at its subject matter. Besides the superb color photographs, the invertebrates are so clearly described that you should have no trouble conclusively identifying any one of the 161 shallow-water marine creatures discussed. The book also includes drawings of each phylum and class. A glossary and a descriptive key to the phyla and classes of invertebrates are included. Both books are available through: Sea Challengers, 1851 Don Ave., Los Osos, CA 93402.

An interesting approach to fish identification is used in the *Handguide to the Coral Reef Fishes of the Caribbean,* by F. Joseph Stokes, illustrated by Charlotte C. Stokes. A quick-reference section classifies fish according to a number of categories including color, markings, body shapes, fin size and shape, spines, habitat, and behavior. This extensive breakdown should make it extremely easy to identify almost all of the 460 species covered in this book. In addition to identification information, the book includes other useful tidbits such as an explanation of why the water is clearer in the tropics than in the temperate zones. Available through: Lippincott and Crowell, 10 E. 53 St., New York, NY 10022.

Pacific Coast Subtidal Marine Invertebrates

A FISHWATCHERS' GUIDE

Daniel W. Gotshall
Laurence L. Laurent

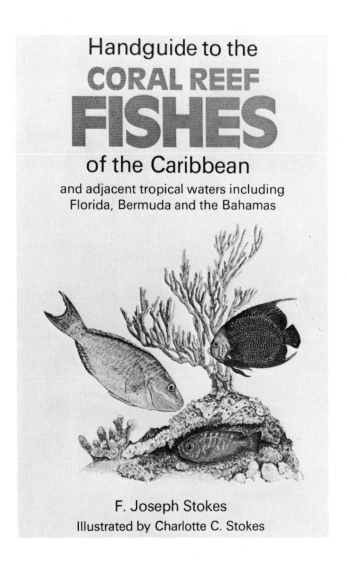

Handguide to the
CORAL REEF
FISHES
of the Caribbean
and adjacent tropical waters including Florida, Bermuda and the Bahamas

F. Joseph Stokes
Illustrated by Charlotte C. Stokes

PHOTOGRAPHY

The Nikonos is a sophisticated 35mm camera designed for use under water without housing. It may be used with or without an underwater automatic flash unit, and at depths much greater than snorkelers usually go. This is an expensive and specialized piece of equipment.

The Minolta Weathermatic is a good 110-type camera for use in or around water. It will take pictures in water as deep as 15 feet, making it ideal for snorkelers.

The thrill of exploring the underwater domain can be relived and shared with friends through photographs. Until a few years ago, underwater photography was hopelessly complex. Today, new cameras and films make capturing the animals and plants of this new world easy and exciting.

Cameras

A number of waterproof cameras are available, from simple pocket types to larger models that use 35 mm film. In addition, several companies manufacture weatherproof housings in which non-waterproof cameras may be carried under water.

Housings

If you already own a quality pocket camera or 35mm camera, you may want to consider one of these housings. A large camera store or diving equipment store will either stock them or have catalogs that show them. The largest manufacture of rigid plastic housings for both pocket and 35mm cameras is Ikelite Underwater Systems. Ikelite makes cases for most brands of pocket cameras. Models such as the Vivitar 118 with a built-in flash or the Kodak Ektralite produce excellent results. Larger pocket cameras such as the older Kodak Instamatics can be used as well. If you buy a housing for a camera that does not have built-in flash, be sure you get the auxilary pieces that will allow you to use flashcubes in the water.

Ikelite's housings for 35mm cameras accomodate most brands currently available including Canon, Nikon, Olympus, Minolta, Vivitar, and Mamiya. Using a 35mm camera with a housing is slightly more complicated than using a pocket-type camera, as the controls of the camera must be manipulated by means of gears and levers. These larger housings are also quite buoyant, thus making it a bit difficult to drag the camera under water while snorkeling. The Ikelite housings produce excellent results, and are used by many professional underwater photographers.

Submersible cameras

Several manufacturers make cameras designed to be waterproof for use under water. Most use either 110-sized film or 35mm film. The 35mm cameras are the more sophisticated—and expensive—but some 110 cameras produce very good results.

The best all-around sports and snorkeling 110-type camera available is the Minolta Weathermatic A, a flat, rectangular yellow camera with a built-in flash unit. The Weathermatic will not leak even at depths to 15 meters (50 ft.), although it may not operate below 4.5 meters (15 ft.). Minolta designed the Weathermatic as an all-sports camera that functions equally well in the water, at the beach, and in snow—anywhere dirt, water, or cold weather might harm an ordinary camera. The Weathermatic is widely available and relatively inexpensive.

Other manufacturers, notably Fujica and Ricoh, make compact submersible 35mm cameras. More expensive than the Weathermatic, the 35mm models also make better photographs. If you want to buy one of these cameras go to a professional camera store for guidance.

Nikonos

The submersible camera used by most professionals is the Nikonos, a 35mm model manufactured by Nikon. There have been four models of this camera, numbered I through IV, the IV-A being the latest. Interchangeable lenses of 15mm, 28mm, 35mm (the camera's "normal" lens) and 80mm are available. Of these, only the 35mm and the 80mm can also be used above water. The Nikonos IV has many advanced features, such as automatic exposure control. If you require professional-quality photos, you will need a Nikonos.

Many underwater photographers put their regular 35mm cameras into waterproof housings. These housings allow you to attach an underwater flash unit if desired.

Because you may not frame your picture directly through the lens of a camera in a housing, you may want to use an external viewfinder for this purpose.

Taking Pictures

The water poses special problems for photographers. First, water absorbs light. Although the effect on the intensity of light will be negligible at the depths you'll be in while snorkeling, the effect on the colors will be noticeable. Reds are lost at depths over 3 meters (10 ft.) below the surface. Although your brain compensates to a degree for this loss of color, the film will not, and your photos will have a blue-green cast unless you use flash to compensate for the loss of red wavelengths from the sunlight.

The easiest way to do this is by using a camera such as the Minolta Weathermatic, which has a built-in flash attachment. Ikelite housings for other cameras have adapters that let you use flash attachments while in the water. For 35mm cameras in housings, or for the Nikonos, several manufacturers (Ikelite, Subsea, Nikon, Oceanic/ Farallon, Sonic Research) make submersible flash units that do not require housing.

Even when the sun is very bright, use the flash attachment unless you are less than 1 meter (3 ft.) under water.

Focusing. Everything you see through your mask under water is slightly magnified and appears closer than it actually is. Most cameras have to be focused by estimating the distance from camera to subject. The easiest way to deal with this is to photograph only subjects that are within arm's reach, about 1 meter (3 ft.) away. At an effective *f*-stop of *f*/5.6, a flashcube or built-in electronic flash will not give good reds at distances greater than 2 meters (6 ft.). Due to absorption, only very powerful flash units such as the Subsea 225 will carry over 1.25 meters (4 ft.). Set your camera's focus ring or dial on its closest setting, and move to that distance from the subject. This will help single out one fish, coral, or other subject in the picture, separating it from the confusing jumble of colors and textures on the reef.

Focusing a camera underwater is more difficult than in air, because of the distortion created by the water. If possible, practice focusing and working the other controls of your camera in a swimming pool before you take it on a snorkeling trip, so you will not miss any exciting shots.

Film

The best film to use in under water photography is Kodacolor II print film. Professional photographers normally use a slide film such as Kodachrome or Ektachrome, but they have the skills and equipment to make sure they expose the film properly. You can also get faster (more light-sensitive) print films than Kodacolor II, which is ISO 100/21°, but as a beginner you will make better pictures sooner using the slower print film.

Although your camera and equipment may seem really heavy and cumbersome on land, they become practically weightless once you get into the water. You may even find some of your equipment floats more easily than you do.

Subjects

Try to pick out one central subject in your photos, concentrating on a fish, a sea fan, a piece of coral, or a shell. Fish move quickly, but make colorful subjects. If you spread a little food around, the fish will stay in the area long enough for you to catch them in your viewfinder. Most corals are either green or purplish-blue, though the shapes make up for their lack of color. Sponges are often bright orange, deep purple, pink, green, or yellow, and make colorful accents to a reef photo. Take pictures of other snorkelers as they explore; wait at the bottom as they come down from above, then frame them against the blue water when they get close. *Do not* chase rays, eels, lobsters, or barracudas with your camera.

How to. Before you dive with your camera, make sure the film is advanced and the camera ready to fire. Check the flashcube to be sure a fresh bulb is ready, or if you have electronic flash, see that the ready light is glowing.

Pick out your subject, inhale, and dive as straight down as you can. Level off at the bottom, kick slowly, and let out a little air, if necessary, to keep from floating up. As you come in on the subject, look through the viewfinder, glide in, and, as you come within 1 meter (3 ft.) of the subject, push the shutter release. Continue up and wind the camera at the surface. When you feel more comfortable with snorkeling, you may want to try going to the bottom, exhaling until you no longer tend to drift up. If you have to, find a piece of non-living coral rock to hang onto to steady yourself. This way, you'll be able to frame your subject slowly, waiting for fish to get into the best position for a shot.

Watch out! While you are concentrating on looking at things through the viewfinder, you may pay less attention to where your arms and legs are. It's terribly easy to back into a patch of fire coral or bump into a coral boulder. Be aware of where your arms and legs are, and of where these obstacles are. Don't let your concentration on getting pictures keep you from looking 360 degrees as you surface.

What subject you focus on underwater will depend on your interests, but whether it is other snorkelers, the corals, or the fish, pictures are a good way to share your experience.

Hints for better photos

- Use Kodacolor π print film.
- Use a little food to attract fish, then photograph them.
- Wear gloves so you can grab rocks to steady yourself at the bottom.
- Carry plenty of flashcubes; if you have a flash unit, carry spare batteries.
- Flashcubes float!
- Keep extra cubes in a small net bag tied to your waist, put used cubes back in the bag and discard them on shore.
- Do not discard anything on the reef.

Getting good pictures of fish means that you will first have to study them a bit to learn how to approach them and how close you can get. This stoplight parrotfish was about 2 feet from the photographer when the picture was made.

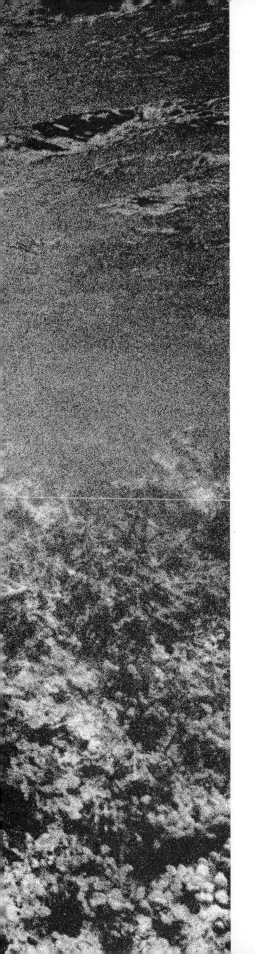

7 | Breathing
Weights and vest
Wetsuits

Advanced
Free Diving

BREATHING

Some of the most enjoyable snorkel activities, especially photography and shelling, are enhanced by the ability to dive under and stay down for a minute or more. At first, you'll find staying down for a full minute taxing, but with practice, and some of the techniques described in this chapter, you can extend your underwater excursions to several minutes each.

Before the advent of compressed air in the nineteenth century, all diving was free diving, done by holding the breath. Aristotle reports that Alexander the Great descended into the sea (perhaps in a diving bell) to watch his divers dismantle underwater defenses in the harbor at Tyre in 332 B.C. Herodotus wrote of an even earlier use of divers, by the Persian King Xerxes, to recover sunken treasure in the fifth century B.C. Spanish priests wrote that Indian divers used by the Spanish to recover cargo from sunken treasure ships in the Americas in the sixteenth century could stay under four minutes on a single breath.

Proper breath control can help make getting below the surface easy.

Breath control

The first and most obvious way to extend your dives is through better breath control. Unless you jog, perform aerobic exercises, practice yoga, or otherwise regularly work out your heart and lungs, chances are your breathing is inefficient. An adult's lungs may hold a total volume of 4.75 liters (10 pints) of air. Under ordinary circumstances, you move only a few pints in and out as you breathe. Of this, your body may recover and use approximately 1 liter 2 ½ pints of oxygen. There is also a residual volume, some space in the lungs which remains filled with air no matter how vigorously you exhale. Your aerobic capacity is the volume of oxygen you are able to absorb and use in one minute. The better your aerobic capacity, the better a free diver you will be. Build up your aerobic capacity and breath control through exercise or yoga.

Hyperventilation

Hyperventilation—breathing in and out deeply several times before a free dive—is another way to extend your time under water. *Read this section carefully and understand it before attempting to hyperventilate.*

Up to now, your dives have been limited in duration by the urgent feeling of having to breathe. This urge to breathe is *not* caused by a lack of oxygen in your lungs; rather, it is caused primarily by the presence of carbon dioxide, the main by-product of your respiration.

You already know that breathing rapidly will allow you to hold your breath longer by postponing the urge to breathe. *Hyperventilation does not increase the amount of oxygen in your lungs or in your blood.* The body has no appreciable capacity to store oxygen. When you hyperventilate, you are actually lowering the amount of carbon dioxide in your system. Your body then takes longer to build up a level of carbon dioxide that will trigger the breathing reflex. During this prolonged period, your body continues to use oxygen that may cause you to lose consciousness.

The safe way

Hyperventilation can be used for free diving if you are cautious. First, before hyperventilating, be sure you are rested, not breathing heavily. Force as much air out of your lungs as you can, pushing with your diaphragm muscles to squeeze the lungs. Now inhale, slowly, as deeply as you can, filling your lungs beyond their normal capacity. Repeat this cycle twice more, for a total of three breaths. Hold the last lungful of air and make your dive.

Never take more than three breaths. More than three breaths may postpone the urge to breathe so long that you will black out from lack of oxygen before you feel the need for air. When you surface, do not pant, but take in full, deep breaths. The level of oxygen in your blood will be low, and it takes time for your body to rebuild blood oxygen. Rest at the surface, breathing deeply, at least two full minutes before attempting another dive.

WEIGHTS AND VEST

Especially if you intend to use weights while snorkeling, you will need an inflatable vest. To be useful, the vest must have an easy way to get air in and out. The vest shown here has a valve in the end of the accordion hose. Pushing in on the rubber mouthpiece opens a valve that allows air to pass in or out. This vest also has a carbon dioxide cartridge for emergency inflation.

One of the chief difficulties in free diving is getting from the surface to the bottom to begin a dive. In the distant past, divers sometimes held rocks in their arms until they reached the bottom, then released them in order to resurface. Aside from the problem of finding and carrying rocks, this method leaves much to be desired: the descent may be too rapid to allow you to equalize your ears on the way down.

Today, weights that attach to a web belt are used by divers. The belt has a quick-release buckle that allows the weights to be dropped quickly and easily in an emergency. You can purchase weights and weight belts from a store that carries scuba diving equipment. There are many types of weights available: cylindrical, flat, rectangular. Get the type that feels best against your body. You will only need a few pounds; remember, you'll be swimming and floating with the weights on as well as diving.

Vest

If you use weights, you will need a small, orally inflatable vest to float you in the water. If you are weighted, you can inflate the vest as you swim on the surface, letting air out to dive. The vest should have 7–9 kilometers (15–20 pounds) of flotation, an easy way to get air in and out, and a 16-gram CO_2 cartridge for emergency inflation. The cartridge will release CO_2 into the vest when a cord is pulled, inflating the vest to float you should be unable to blow air into it. CO_2 cartridges are not completely reliable because the mechanism that punctures the cartridge tends to corrode. Don't rely on the CO_2 to save you. However, having a cartridge that might work is better than having none at all.

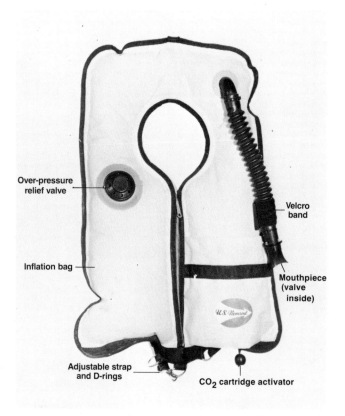

Over-pressure relief valve

Velcro band

Inflation bag

Mouthpiece (valve inside)

U.S. Divers

Adjustable strap and D-rings

CO_2 cartridge activator

Using weights and vest

When using weights and a vest, it is best to practice with them in a swimming pool or other safe water area before trying them in the open ocean. The feeling of diving with weights is totally different from ordinary diving.

In putting on a vest and weights, the weights always go on last. The weight belt goes over everything else you're wearing, with the quick-release buckle positioned in front of you. Should you need to drop the weights, it is essential that the belt come away cleanly, without tangling under or in other straps, your vest, or anything else attached to your body.

There are many kinds of weight belts and weights available. All belts should have a quick-release buckle so you can "dump" the belt easily if you must make a fast ascent. Weights are usually made of lead cast in various configurations or as buckshot to be used with a channeled belt.

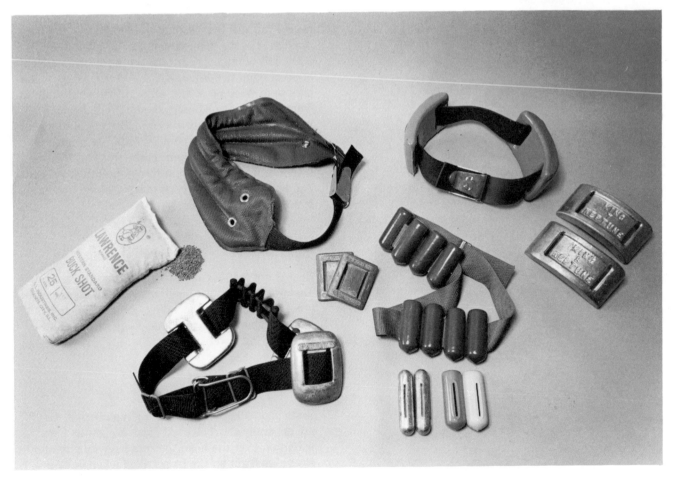

WETSUITS

If the water is cool, or if you are planning on spending more than 15 or 20 minutes in even tropical water, you'll need some kind of protection to keep from being chilled. Water conducts heat away from the body much faster than air does. A water temperature of 21C (70°F) can quickly become quite uncomfortable, while an air temperature of 21C feels very nice.

A unique material, neoprene, has been developed to keep swimmers, divers, skiiers, and surfers warm. Neoprene is a synthetic rubber material in which small bubbles of gas have been trapped. The bubbles give the neoprene a texture like foam rubber. Neoprene garments keep your body warm by trapping a thin layer of water next to your body. Body heat warms the water, and very little heat is lost through the insulating neoprene.

Generally, in water below 15C (60°F) you will need a full suit (pants, long-sleeved jacket, and hood) of 6mm (1¼ in.) neoprene. From 18–21C (65–70°F), a full suit of 3mm (⅛ in.) neoprene, or torso and hood of 6mm neoprene, will do. Above 21C, you may choose to wear no suit at all or, if you chill easily, a 3mm shorty suit or jacket should do. Individual metabolisms and body weight make vast differences in how people are affected by water temperatures. Thin divers will need more protection than heavier divers, and men need more protection than women. The length of time in the water is also an important factor.

Heat loss

Heat is not lost evenly through all parts of the body. The areas of greatest heat loss (and most in need of protection) are, in descending order; head, groin, torso, armpits, arms, and legs. Keep this in mind when buying a wetsuit.

Vests and jackets

Vests and jackets are waist-length garments. Vests are generally short sleeved or sleeveless and are pulled on over the head. Jackets have long or short sleeves and zip up the front. A "chicken vest" is a

Neoprene vests can help conserve body heat. They are available for men or women, and they may or may not have sleeves.

vest with hood attached. These are very comfortable, and the short-sleeved versions do not hamper the movement of your arms.

Farmer john

The farmer john is a pair of pants that comes up under a vest or jacket like a pair of bib overalls. Although the farmer john has been very popular with surfers, by itself it isn't the best protection for snorkelers. It covers primarily the legs, an area of low heat loss.

Shorty suit

A shorty suit is a short-sleeved suit that covers the torso from neck to groin and zips up the front. Usually 3mm (⅛ in.) or 4.5mm (³⁄₁₆ in.) thick, it is good protection for water above 21C (70°F).

Full suit

A full suit may be pants and jacket (long sleeves and legs), or a one-piece garment like a jumpsuit.

Materials

Manufacturers of neoprene suits have their own language. The neoprene itself is referred to as "skin." Neoprene is black and is not slippery, making it difficult to slide into pants or a jacket. So manufacturers now cover one or both sides of the neoprene with nylon fabric or some other synthetic, such as lycra, which makes the garment much easier to get on or off and more comfortable. If both sides are coated, you can also get a selection of attractive colors.

If the garment is neoprene only, it is known as "S2S" or "skin" (neoprene) on two sides. N1S means that one side is faced with nylon, while N2S means a nylon covering inside and out. N2S garments are by far the most comfortable and durable.

Wetsuits change your buoyancy

Wearing a suit will cause you to float, due to the buoyancy of the gas bubbles in the neoprene. You will almost certainly need weights if you wear a wetsuit. The thicker the suit, and the more of your body it covers, the more weight you'll need to dive.

The full suit shown here is a two-piece set—jacket with long sleeves and pants with long legs—that provides maximum thermal protection, especially when used with accessories such as the neoprene boots shown. One-piece full suits are also available.

8 | **Learning scuba**
Types of diving
The first step

Scuba

LEARNING SCUBA

Ditching and donning
equipment under water
builds confidence.

To extend your time under water to more than a minute or two, you will need a supply of air to take with you. A piece of equipment to do just that, the aqualung, was invented in 1943 by Jacques Cousteau and Emile Gagnan. Called SCUBA (Self-Contained Underwater Breathing Apparatus), the aqualung consists of a tank of pressurized air, a tank valve, a pressure-sensitive valve called a regulator, and a mouthpiece. When used with the basic snorkeling gear, it enables divers to go down 30 meters (100 ft.) or more for a few minutes, or to depths of 15 meters for about an hour.

Using pressurized air and an aqualung is more complicated than snorkeling because of the various effects of increased pressure on your body. As noted earlier, in water, the pressure doubles at 10 meters (33 ft.), and increases by 0.4 kilograms per square centimeter (14.7 lbs. per sq. in.) with each additional 10 meters of depth.

It is necessary to be taught scuba by a certified instructor. Various private agencies (see box) license instructors. You can be sure of the quality of instruction if the teacher holds a certificate from one of these agencies. Facilities that rent or sell scuba gear, and that fill scuba tanks, will not rent you scuba gear or fill a tank if you do not have a certification card (known as a C-Card) from one of the recognized agencies to prove that you have completed a course of training in the proper use of scuba.

In the 1950s it was customary to begin diving instruction by being admonised not to hold your breath and come up at the same time. Then you were turned loose with a set of gear. Since then, a lot of information has been developed which makes learning easier and brings proficiency faster: how to handle the equipment, time and depth limits, how to get on or off a boat, how to achieve weightlessness.

The two most popular ways to learn to dive are to take a course at a local dive shop or YMCA, or to go to a watersports resort that teaches diving. By

Buddy-breathing is one of
the training exercises
practiced when learning to
scuba dive.

taking the course in your hometown, you'll end up a certified diver, able to rent equipment and dive unsupervised just about anywhere. The disadvantage is that, unless you live near the tropics, your first dive is likely to be in dark, cold water with low visibility. Like hiking Monument Valley on a moonless night, it's exciting just to be there not knowing what's around you. But then, you'll never really know what *was* around you.

Taking the course at a tropical watersports resort gives you the choice of taking a very short (hours- or days-long) course that qualifies you to dive with an instructor's supervision, or of taking a longer full course. The advantage here is that you learn to dive in a real, hands-on environment. Lessons will be less formal and followed immediately by practice in warm, clear water. On your first or second afternoon, you'll be looking at corals and colorful tropical fish—the fun stuff. The disadvantage is that you'll spend one or more days of your vacation in a classroom.

The world opened to you through the use of scuba equipment is nothing short of fantastic. The glowing adjectives used by Jules Verne in *Twenty Thousand Leagues Beneath the Sea* can scarcely do justice to the multiplicity of forms, riotous colors and profusion of life under water. The aquatic world includes animals (such as anemones) that look like plants, plants that look like rocks, animals that look like rocks; a petting zoo of protein so complex that even marine biologists have a hard time sorting out which creatures belong to which kingdom. Your ticket into this natural amusement park is the air tank and regulator. At depths of 15 or 18 meters (50 or 60 ft.) huge banks of coral grow in warm tropical seas; rock ledges hide shy, colorful fish in freshwater lakes; and shipwrecks from rowboats to ocean liners beckon.

Scuba Training Agencies

There are several international organizations that license diving instructors. Look for their emblems wherever you decide to try diving. These agencies also supply the names of specific teachers either near your home or at some travel destination.

British Sub-Aqua Club (BSAC)
70 Brompton Road
London SW31HA
United Kingdom
Telephone: (0) 584-7163

Confédération Mondiale des Activités Subaquatiques (CMAS)
32 rue du Colisée
75008 Paris, France
Telephone: 225-60-42

National Association of Scuba Diving Schools (NASDS)
P.O. Box 17067
Long Beach, CA 90807
Telephone: (213) 595-5361

National Association of Underwater Instructors (NAUI)
4650 Arrow Highway
Montclair, CA 91763
Telephone: (714) 621-5801

National YMCA Underwater Activities Program
P.O. Box 1547
Key West, FL 33040
Telephone: (305) 294-5288

Professional Association of Diving Instructors (PADI)
2064 N. Bush Street
Santa Ana, CA 92706
Telephone: (714) 547-6996

Learning to move through tight spaces is good training for wreck and cave diving.

TYPES OF DIVING

Scuba divers often characterize different types of diving by referring to the environment the dive is done in—wall diving, current diving, river diving, wreck diving, and night diving are all common expressions.

Wall diving

A wall is an underwater cliff. It may be the submerged part of a dry land formation or a dropoff some distance from shore. In coral areas, cliffs are usually covered with growths of sponges, soft and hard corals, sea fans and other attached marine life. Fish, small and large, move in and around the growth. Swimming backwards, away from the wall, the bottom drops away until only a deep indigo color can be seen below. From this vantage point, the wall resembles an enormous organic tapestry of varied colors and textures. Often a strong current runs parallel to the wall; this allows divers to combine their wall diving with current diving. Hitching a ride in the flow of water, the diver is swept along with the current. The wall ambles by, presenting an ever-changing mosaic of life.

Diving on the rock walls that are found under water in some cold-water areas, such as the New England coast, Puget Sound in Washington state, or Vancouver in British Columbia, can be exciting, too. The cool, nutrient-rich waters in these areas encourage the growth of soft corals, anemones and nudibranchs—a colorful marine relative of the slug. Anemones in these areas may be four to five times the size of those found in tropical waters, and have a greater range of colors. The pink, or strawberry, anemones are particularly beautiful.

Gliding effortlessly up the steep slope of a coral reef is a joyful and exciting experience.

Wreck diving

There is something mysterious about a shipwreck, something hard to resist. At first blush, swimming around or into a sunken boat might be a little scary, but once you've tried it, it's like exploring an abandoned house. In many places, large ships have been sunk intentionally to create artificial reefs to attract fish. These wrecks are usually thoroughly cleared of dangerous debris before being sunk and are quite safe for divers. Most of the larger wrecks are simple steel freighters, but every water area has at least one or two special wrecks. In Lake Ontario near Tobermory, Ontario, are several large, wooden freighters from the late nineteenth century. The fresh lake water has preserved the wood more or less intact. Wooden wrecks in the ocean are attacked by tiny teredo worms and tend to disintegrate more rapidly. In the Mediterranean and certain areas of the Pacific, such as Truk Lagoon, divers can explore the intact remains of World War II fighter planes. At Truk, the scene of one of the crucial naval battles of the war, a number of Japanese freighters and war ships were sunk. The tanks, trucks, airplanes, and supplies they carried are still on their decks or scattered around the bottom in clear, warm water.

Night diving

Just as there are some land animals that only come out at night, there are many marine animals that are primarily nocturnal. Coral reefs, in particular, are more active at night than during the day. After the sun goes down, the coral polyps emerge to feed, giving the hard corals (that look like rocks during the day) a furry texture, like shag carpeting. Octopuses, which hide in holes in the reef during the day, come out to feed and can often be seen slinking through the coral. Especially in some tropical areas, there are plankton that become phosphorescent when disturbed; a diver moving through the water leaves a fiery trail flowing from fin tips and fingers. With hand lights turned off and a full moon above, the underwater landscape is bathed in an ethereal pearl-blue glow.

The chance to discover a wreck under water is a great adventure and the prime reason why many divers go under water.

THE FIRST STEP

These and other scuba experiences are available to anyone in reasonably good health. The first step is to visit a retail store in your area that sells scuba diving equipment and offers instruction sanctioned by one of the certification agencies in the box on page 105. After you've completed the basic course, you may want to continue into the specialty courses the various agencies offer. These allow you to ease into more advanced types of scuba diving—wreck diving, night diving, perhaps even ice diving beneath a frozen lake—with an experienced and certified instructor to help. If you enjoyed the snorkeling experiences in this book, chances are you'll love scuba diving.

Encountering nature under water is much easier than on land. Curious creatures often come in close to give the new visitor a careful examination.

APPENDIX: BASIC LIFE SAVING

Getting a Victim out of the Water

If someone gets in trouble in the water, you may have to go to the rescue. This is quite simple if you take a few precautions. First, never approach a drowning person from the front. A panicky victim is likely to react by grabbing you with both hands, probably around the neck, making it impossible for you to swim and possibly forcing you under. Instead, circle around behind the victim and get one hand across his chest. If you find you can't get behind the victim, or if he manages to get his hands on you and starts to drag you down, make a fist and punch him sharply in the diaphragm—right in the V-shaped space between the bottom of the two sides of the ribs and above the stomach. When he quits fighting you, tow him in.

Chin tow. To tow a tired swimmer, get behind him, turn him on his back, and grasp him by cupping one hand under chin. You will be under him, more or less, supporting his head and upper back on one hip. Using a gentle side stroke, tow him in.

Chest tow. The chest tow is similar to the chin tow. Get the swimmer on his back, but instead of grasping his chin, get your arm over his shoulder, across his chest, and under his armpit on the other side. The chest tow gives you better control of the victim then does the chin tow.

Artificial respiration

If a drowning victim has stopped breathing, you'll have to perform mouth to mouth resuscitation.

First, turn the victim onto his back and, if necessary, quickly wipe out his mouth. Place one hand under the victim's neck and lift, tilting the head back as far as possible with the other hand. This provides an airway (see illustration A).

If the victim is not breathing, pinch his nostrils shut (illustration B), take a deep breath, place your mouth lightly over his mouth, allowing the victim to exhale. If you can't force air into the lungs, the airway may be blocked. Roll the victim over and strike him hard between the shoulderblades to dislodge anything in his throat, then try again.

Give four breaths and check for neck pulse. If a pulse is present, continue rescue breathing at 12 times a minute (count to five between each breath you give). If the victim is a small child or infant, cover both his nose and mouth with your mouth, and blow gently 20 times a minute (count to 3 between each breath).

Feel for the victim's neck pulse. Keeping head tilted with one hand, use your middle and index fingers of the other hand to feel for the carotid pulse under the side angle of the lower jaw. If there is no pulse, continue rescue breathing and start cardiopulmonary resuscitation (CPR).

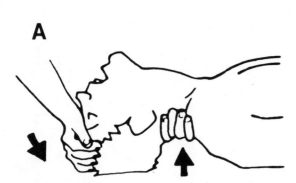

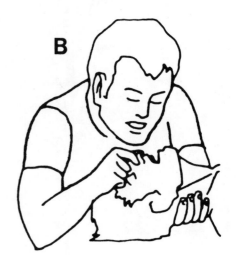

Cardiopulmonary resuscitation

CPR should not normally be attempted by someone who has not had specific training, since its incorrect application may do more harm than good. On the other hand, if there is no pulse and the victim cannot breathe on his own, and *if no other help is available*, an untrained person may have no other course of action.

The victim's back should be on a firm surface. For an adult victim, place the heel of one hand on the lower breastbone (about 1½ in. [4cm]) up from the tip, with fingers off the chest; place your other hand on top, and rock gently forward, exerting pressure down 1½–2 inches to force blood out of the heart. Release pressure. Alternate artificial respiration with CPR (illustration C).

If there is only one rescuer, you must perform both activities. Give the victim 80 compressions a minute, with two full breaths after each 15 compressions. If there are two rescuers, one should give 60 chest compressions a minute, while the other gives one breath after each five compressions.

If the victim is a child, you must apply less pressure to the chest than you would to an adult. For an infant, use only the tips of your index and middle finger of one hand, over the center of the breastbone. Depress chest lightly only ½ to ¾ of an inch (1.27 to 1.9cm). Give 80 to 100 compressions a minute, and

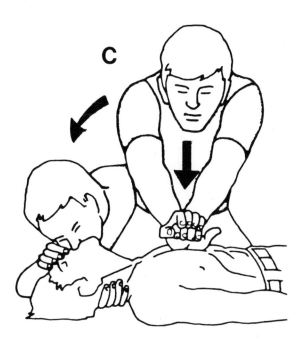

one breath after each five compressions. For a small child, use only the heel of one hand over the center of the breastbone. Depress the chest ¾ to 1½ inches (1.9 to 4.0cm). Give 800 to 100 compressions a minute, and one breath after each five compressions.

The above information and accompanying art were adapted from a brochure published by the Metropolitan Life Insurance Company

INDEX